MAN IN HOLE

Love, Lies, Addiction, and Butting Porcupines

BY

DOUG DODD

ISBN Number: 978-1-59433-806-9
eBook ISBN Number: 978-1-59433-807-6

—First Edition—

Manufactured in the United States of America

CONTENTS

Acknowledgements 5
Introduction 6

1. Butting Porcupines 7
2. Helpless and Useless 10
3. My Position at the Mission 16
4. Beginnings 20
5. Savage Summers 23
6. Leaving Home 31
7. Cooking for Jesus 36
8. Off to See the Wizard 40
9. Tripping 46
10. Called to Serve 53
11. The Lost Years 57
12. Sinner-man, where You Gonna Run To? 61
13. Pants on Fire in Portland 68
14. I Walk the Line 71
15. Life at the Lazy W 75
16. Time, Not Entirely Wasted 81
17. Eruption and Extinction 85
18. The Climbing Fool 91

19. Get a Job! 97
20. Raised by Wolffs 101
21. Avalanche! 105
22. Hot Coffee at the Lazy W 110
23. Down in Flames 114
24. I'll Burn that Bridge when I Get to It 119
25. Déjà vu All Over Again 123
26. Backsliding into Recovery 129
27. The 55 Year Old Greenhorn 134
28. The Plant, the Village, the Island 141
29. Conversation and Cows 148
30. The Hills Go on Forever 151
31. Wreckage from My Past 156
32. Cattle, Confusion and Change 161
33. The Write Stuff for a Miracle 167
34. Fools Rush In 171
35. A Homer Surprise 176
36. Facing the Elephant with Walter and Leola 179
37. Ammends, Where Possible 187
38. The Best of Times 192
39. Cancer and Empathy 195
40. Hello Dad, and Goodbye 200
41. Full Circle 209

Afterward 217

ACKNOWLEDGEMENTS

This book is the result of a lot of help from many people. Thanks to Julie and Greg, and Kermit and Carol. Each of you became a friend to the friendless and gave me your undeserved trust when I needed it most. Nate and Tiffany, thanks for giving me permission to share parts of your stories, and for forgiving me my many trespasses. To Tim and Ela, my two professional readers, thanks for your caring honesty, surely a difficult line to walk, yet you both stepped with consummate care. Nadya, I am grateful for the council, currants and conversation we shared. Thanks to everyone in my writers group for your encouragement and the consistently superior snacks. Thanks to Publications Consultants for taking the pain out of publishing. Finally, I am grateful to the Cow Woman for never allowing me to give up. This book is for her.

INTRODUCTION

For thirty-three years my longest period of continuous sobriety never exceeded two months. In 1986, during my first stint in rehab, a counselor asked me to name my drug of choice. My reply, ‘whatever you've got”, was flippant, but the joke was on me. By that time my denial had shifted from “I can quit any time, I just don't want to,” to “I'm an addict and I can't quit, so why try?”

By the end of 2000, I had got high thousands of times rather than face things about myself that I didn't like. I had made bad choices and refused to take responsibility for them. I had cast myself as a victim in my own melodrama, and I was sick of it. It was time for a change and I was ready.

CHAPTER 1
BUTTING PORCUPINES

MARCH 7, 1996 YAKIMA, WASHINGTON

I step out the kitchen door, duck my head against a stinging blast of icy snow, and sprint across the courtyard through the drifts. I am late again, and the chapel is packed with a dozen Program men and twice that many homeless clients, the latter hoping to postpone their inevitable exit into the freak spring blizzard that dropped half a foot of snow overnight. I have been up since five helping the new cook with breakfast. I should be training him on lunch, but attendance at the morning service is compulsory for all men in the Program – even for me, the food service manager. I am almost in my chair when Rick Phillips speaks.

"So glad you could join us, Doug. Come on up, it's your turn to deliver today's message. Our topic this morning is 'besetting sin'. Besetting sin," he continues, "is a specific, repeated sin to which a person is especially vulnerable, something I think you can relate to." Rick leans back in his chair, folds his arms and purses his lips.

Rick is the Mission Director, the top dog, and to the Southern Baptists who staff the place, on a par with Moses. I've been in the Program for almost four months, so I've been expecting this. Rick eventually asks every man in the New Life Program to deliver a morning message. Usually he lets a man pick his own topic or suggests something general like 'salvation' or 'God's love'. Today I feel ambushed and have no idea where to begin. As I walk slowly to the podium, forty-year-old memories of my boyhood flood my head. I take a long breath and hold it. I open my mouth and the words come out.

"I grew up deep in the mountains of Montana. Our ranch was on Butler Creek, a tiny stream you've probably never heard of, where we ran cattle and sheep. One summer, when I was eleven or twelve, my father bought a buck sheep - a ram - at auction. That ram was mean. He charged people and butted them from behind." A couple clients snicker and Rick frowns. These morning mini-sermons are supposed to edify, not entertain, but I have an idea where I'm headed and forge ahead.

"We tried to break him of this habit, but it was no use. Sheep have very hard heads, and this buck was big, almost two-hundred pounds. If he hit you, you went down. No matter what we did, he kept butting. Dad worried someone might get hurt bad, so we isolated the ram in a separate pasture. One day he didn't come to his feed and Dad sent me to see what was wrong." Everyone is watching now - clients, Program men, even Rick.

"When I got close I could see porcupine quills sticking out of his face so I ran and told my folks. While Mom and I held the ram down, Dad went to work with needle-nose pliers. There were dozens of quills – too many to count – from nose to tail and everywhere in between. We figured the ram charged, the porky curled into a ball, and the ram ran right over him. It was a bloody mess, and the buck thrashed and bleated in agony. We had to do it, before the barbed quills worked their way in, hit a vital organ, and killed him." Some of the clients appear to be holding their breath.

"You might think that buck learned his lesson and quit butting, right? Nope. Next week he butted my grandfather, and we had to put the ram back in solitary. A couple weeks later, we found him dead with a broken neck. The carcass was partly eaten, with bear tracks around the kill. We figured he tried to butt one last time." I pause and run my eyes over my audience.

"That ram suffered pain and eventually died because he was too stubborn to change. He was just a dumb sheep so there was no sin involved, but he was still dead. For thirty years, I was like that ram, using drugs and butting my head against God's law, helpless to stop. I have an immortal soul, so I was beset by sin. Because of Jesus's sacrifice, I don't have to share that ram's fate, and neither do you. Amen!" The chapel is silent as I stand at the podium waiting for Rick's reaction.

He leaves without a word, and I head back to the kitchen. A few minutes later, one of the secretaries speaks over the intercom.

"All Program men report to the library. Program men to the library immediately."

It's time to pee in a cup – again. Today is Thursday. They have never done a U.A. on a weekend, so I can party tonight and piss clean Monday morning. With my kitchen key I can slip in and out unnoticed. I have forty bucks from a trip to the plasma bank. If I grab a big turkey from the freezer, maybe Miguel will trade me an eight-ball for the bird and my cash. I imagine lighting up a nice big rock. I can almost taste the smoke and feel the rush from that first hit.

Besetting sin, my ass.

Chapter 2

Helpless and Useless

November, 1995 Yakima, Washington

Four months earlier, I'd maxed out all my credit cards, the bank had repossessed car, my utilities were shut off, and my 'friends' had fled. Mary, loyal almost to the end, was the last to leave.

"Doug, I can't make it on the street in this town in the winter. My sister in Pasco says I can stay with her for a while. I like you, but we're bad for each other. You're smart, but you keep on like this, the rock is gonna kill you."

"You're right, Mary, but where am I going to go? My family's given up on me, my friends too. You're the last one. You got money for a bus ticket?"

"My sister sent me a ticket, non-refundable. She knows me too well. Why don't you go down to the Mission, at least for Thanksgiving dinner? I know a guy who lives there off and on and he says it's not too bad if you don't mind the Bible thumping."

"Maybe I will. They're on North First, right?"

"Yeah, hey, you want to give me a hand to the bus with this suitcase?"

That was the last I saw of Mary and as the bus rolled away I hoped her geographical cure would help.

On Thanksgiving morning, I woke up to two feet of fresh snow. By then I weighed about one hundred thirty pounds, but even so I could have earned a little cash clearing sidewalks – if I hadn't already sold the shovel. Instead I huddled in my icy apartment until noon, before bundling up and slogging the dozen blocks to the Union Gospel Mission. I arrived soaked to my knees, feet numb from the cold, only to find that the meal wasn't for another three hours. I hadn't eaten for two days and it was warm in the lobby, so I decided to wait.

The Mission sprawled in what looked like a repurposed motor court with offices and a large dining room to the front. Three wings of rooms, laid out in the shape of a 'U' two stories high, connected to the front offices to create a large inner courtyard. A one story concrete block and glass structure had been added to the rear of the complex, and beyond that lay a fenced yard, its benches now buried in snow.

Almost everything about the rear addition was glass – walls, doors and even the partitions that separated the lobby from two twenty-by-sixty-foot day rooms that resembled giant fish tanks. Each day room contained a podium, a piano, about fifty metal folding chairs and a drinking fountain.

The Mission, run by people Mom would have called 'hard-shell Baptists,' did not allow unsupervised contact between the sexes, so one day room was for single men while the other was for women and children. If a couple was married, and had a certificate to prove it, the husband was allowed limited access to the family area. Before meals there was a service in each dayroom, one in English and one in Spanish.

That Thanksgiving afternoon most of the clientele – bums, drunks, addicts, mental cases and the disabled – hung out in the day rooms, though a few stood outside smoking cigarettes. Almost all the clients were men, and most seemed to know each other. I didn't recall seeing any of them before. I sat alone, head down, silent and very hungry as I tried to dry my sodden boots. When a quiet, faintly southern voice came from behind, I twitched involuntarily.

"Howdy, I don't think we've met." I glanced back and saw jeans topped by a silver belt buckle above a pair of black hand-tooled cowboy boots pointed in my direction. Great. Just what I needed, Cowboy Tex come to save my soul.

"I've never been here before." I kept my voice low. Maybe if I didn't make eye contact he'd go away.

"My name's Aubrey. What brings y'all to the Mission?" I felt my face flush. Did this clown think my presence was part of a well-thought-out career plan? But my mom's training kicked in and I stood up.

"I'm Doug. I guess I'm here for the meal. I hear it's a good one." I took the extended hand and gazed into the eyes of a slim, black haired fellow at least fifteen years my junior. Aubrey's grip was politely firm and his eyes gazed back at me appraisingly.

"Welcome, Doug. The boys in the kitchen sure do try to set a good spread. Glad you're here. You have any questions or need some help, just ask for me at the desk. Okay?" He inclined his head in the direction of the glassed-in cubicle.

"What kind of 'help' are we talking about here, Aubrey?"

"Any old kind at all, Doug, but 'specially the kind Jesus talks about in Mathew 25." I hadn't studied the Bible in over thirty years, so I didn't catch Aubrey's reference.

"Well, thanks for the offer. I'll see how things work out."

"You're welcome and God bless you, Doug." As he turned and walked away I tried to feel superior and failed. Aubrey seemed happy and sincere while I was desperately miserable and surely in need of a blessing.

The pre-meal service lasted about an hour and the meal afterward was traditional American Thanksgiving: turkey, dressing, potatoes, gravy, candied yams, cranberry sauce and pumpkin pie. It wasn't home-made but then I hadn't been home in what felt like forever. By the time I finished stuffing myself, my boots and pants were dry.

On the walk back to my apartment I kept to the middle of the street in the beaten tracks and arrived, only slightly damp, in time to see my soon to be ex-landlord's 4X4 disappearing around the corner. Taped to my door was a final eviction notice (I'd ignored the first one) ordering me to be out the next day. I had almost no possessions, no furniture, no phone – everything I owned would fit in my day pack and single suitcase. Moving would be simple - if I had somewhere to go. I settled in for a cold night and in the morning headed back to see Aubrey.

When I arrived in the Mission lobby, Aubrey greeted me from behind the desk.

"Howdy, Doug, good to see you again. What's going on?"

"I've thought about what you said yesterday, Aubrey, about help, and well, I need some. I'm broke and I'm being evicted from my apartment."

"You can stay here. When do you need to be out?"

"Today. I'm sorry that's not much notice, but…."

"Not a problem, you can stay in the men's dorm tonight. There's two ways we can do this, though. Have you heard about our New Life Program?" I shook my head and he continued.

"Well in that case, you should talk to Ellery Banks." He picked up a phone and dialed. "Hey, Ellery, can you swing by the office? There's someone here to talk to you about the program."

Aubrey hung up and looked at me. "Have a seat, Doug. Ellery will be right over."

A few minutes later, the courtyard door opened and a mocha-colored dude behind a pair of shades and a smile bopped up to me, hand outstretched.

"Hey, Brother, welcome to the Mission. I'm Ellery."

Aubrey and Ellery were country mouse and city cousin, slow talkin' and fast walkin.' Under other circumstances I might have laughed at the contrast, but in this situation they were spiritual tag-team partners, ready to do what was necessary as they wrestled with the devil for another lost soul. Between the two of them, the devil didn't stand a chance and neither did I. Five minutes after Ellery arrived, I was in his office listening to his pitch for the Men's New Life Program.

"Everyone is welcome here, Doug. We have a dorm with fifty-six bunks and twelve two-man rooms. You have a choice of being in the Program or on the Line. Men on the Line get a bunk in the dorm with a shower every night and three meals a day. Dinner's at seven, then it's straight to the dorm for a shower, lights out by nine. Wakeup is at seven a.m. and after breakfast the Line guys take off for the day. Once a week we open the clothing room and hand out clean used clothes. That's it for the Line." Ellery paused, as though expecting a response and I figured there must be a catch.

"That sounds great, Ellery. How much does it cost?"

Ellery blinked in surprise.

"It's all free, Doug, and while it will keep you alive, it's really just for the men who are unable or unwilling to change. It's also very restrictive. For example, the Line guys have to sign up for a bunk every afternoon between one and five and attend chapel at six. Once chapel starts they can't leave the Mission till morning. If a man leaves anyway, he's out for the night, no exceptions. During the day the Line guys can't use any of the facilities except the day room, rest room and back yard." Ellery looked at me, suddenly unsmiling, perhaps seeing the disdain in my face.

"What's your story, Doug?" Ellery's tone had hardened. "Are you happy with your life right now? If you are, don't waste my time. Come back this afternoon and sign up for a bunk."

My face flushed with anger. Who did Ellery think he was, speaking to me this way? I bit back my automatic, sarcastic response. Who was I to take offense? Suddenly my eyes were wet and my mouth was dry.

"No," I managed to croak, "I hate my life. I'm not worth shit to anybody."

"That's not true, Doug," Ellery said softly. "Jesus thought you were worth dying for on the cross. Don't prove him wrong. Are you ready to change?" At my nod, Ellery continued.

"If you join the program you'll live and work right here in the Mission. After a month in the dorm you'll move into a two-man room – they have real beds, by the way. You'll study the scriptures, find a local church, fellowship with Christian brothers, and along the way we'll help you get medical and dental care, anything you need."

I was in shock. Ellery had just offered me food, clothing, shelter, medical care and a job. I'd stubbornly gone my own way ever since I left the ranch and ended up broke, homeless and unemployable. I owed thousands in credit card debt and tens of thousands in back child support. Life at the Mission had to be better than what I'd managed on my own. On November 24, 1995, the day after Thanksgiving, and a week past my fiftieth birthday, I joined the men's program at the Union Gospel Mission.

Chapter 3

My Position at the Mission

December 1995, Yakima, Washington

I never counted the Mission's beds, but there were certainly over one hundred. Some of the staff plus the nine or ten second year trainees lived on site in their own apartments. Program guys like me slept two to a room. The bunks in the family shelter and dorms could accommodate around seventy-five.

The desk was staffed 24-7, the men's dorm operated every night and the laundry ran six days a week. There was daily sweeping and mopping, and the buildings required regular maintenance. The program men and trainees did it all.

Most of the work though, happened in the kitchen. There were two crews, each with a head cook, two cook's helpers and a dishwasher. Two days after I joined the program, I was on the morning crew washing dishes. My shift started at breakfast and didn't end till after lunch. Not everyone staying at the Mission ate with us, but we usually served fifty or sixty at breakfast and lunch. The other crew handled evening meals which usually attracted eighty to one hundred people.

Around eight-thirty one morning, early in December, I was scrubbing a scorched pot when my name came over the intercom.

"Doug Dodd, please report to Ellery Bank's office. Doug Dodd, see Ellery Banks."

"Hey, I'm nearly done here," I called out to Travis, the morning cook. "Ellery wants to see me. I'll leave these pots to soak and finish with them when I get back, alright?"

"Yeah, that's fine," Travis responded. "I'm gonna sack out for a few minutes. Wake me up by 10:30 so I can throw the chili-mac in the oven for lunch, okay?" Chili-mac, a foul, carminative, concoction of canned chili mixed with dry packets of macaroni and cheese, was one of Travis's favorites - probably because all he had to do was dump the ingredients into a six inch pan, add water and shove the result into a 400 degree convection oven for half an hour.

"Sure thing, Trav, no problem." I shucked my apron and headed for Ellery's office.

Outside Ellery's office door, I paused a moment and then knocked. Why did Ellery want to see me? Maybe he could tell I was just faking it, trying my best to fit in, but not really believing all the 'hallelujah' and 'bless you, brother' crap he was selling. I couldn't afford to be kicked out; I had nowhere else to go. Ellery's door popped open and he stood there, an appraising look on his face.

"Come in, I want you to meet someone." He indicated a thin, dark haired man who stood at his side. "Doug, this is Dennis, the kitchen manager. I've been telling him about you."

Shit! Something must be wrong, why else would the manager want to meet a dishwasher? I took Dennis's hand. Behind thick, black framed glasses, space alien eyes gleamed, enlarged and distorted, revealing nothing.

"Pleased to meet you," I mumbled.

"Sit down, Doug." Dennis began, "I've been out of town, just got back yesterday, but I've been hearing things about you and I wanted to meet you myself. How do you like it in the kitchen?" His lips parted in what I guessed was a smile, revealing a flash of yellow teeth.

"It's okay, but I've got a lot to learn."

"You're the dish washer, right?" At my nod, Dennis continued. "I heard that yesterday you prepared the lunch. Is that true?" He wasn't smiling now.

"Yeah, Travis said he was sick about ten yesterday and went back to his room. That left just me and Robbie." Robbie was handicapped; a little guy with a big head. In his fifties, he had a stutter and could barely manage his own hygiene. Robbie had no family and without the mission, he probably would have ended up dying on the street. He was hardworking and honest, but struggled to make even simple decisions, as Dennis certainly knew. I looked Dennis directly in the eye and continued. "Robbie asked me what to do – he was shaking and I could tell he was upset – so I made a salad and grilled a hundred cheese sandwiches. The staff was in a meeting and I didn't know who to call. I know I'm not supposed to fix food, but…." I shrugged but Dennis wasn't quite finished.

"A little bird told me you made the oatmeal this morning. What about that?"

"Travis overslept, and people expect breakfast, so I fixed oatmeal and they ate it. What was I supposed to do?" I could hear the defensive tone in my voice.

Dennis opened his mouth, when Ellery broke in.

"Relax, Doug, you're not in trouble. We're just not used to this, are we Dennis?"

"Ellery's right. Frankly, we don't see this kind of initiative from most of the guys. Have you ever done any cooking?"

"Not really, but I couldn't just sit on my hands." Ellery laughed and looked at Dennis.

"You'd be surprised how good some people are at doing exactly that. Dennis, tell him what you've decided"

"Here's what we're going to do. I'm going to move Travis to the evening shift. He's not a morning person and maybe he'll do better there. Starting tomorrow, I want you to be the morning head cook. Are you okay with that?"

"Yeah, but you need to tell me what you want me to do – meal planning, recipes and stuff."

"Ellery tells me you're supposed to stay in the dorm two more weeks," Dennis ignored my words and continued, "but I've decided to move you into a room this weekend."

"That'll be great. I promise I won't let you down." I was stunned. I'd feared punishment and instead got a promotion. Less than a month later, I understood they were one and the same.

Chapter 4

Beginnings

The Three Bar D ranch, 1950s Montana

By the time I ended up at the mission my mother was fifteen years dead. The cancer, not my bad behavior, had driven her to her grave at fifty-two, but her words still lived in my head.

"I declare, Douglas, you are the most contrary child. Don't give me your uppity backtalk or I'll tan your hide." When she was angry she reverted to her north Texas idiom, and as far back as I can remember she and I were at odds. I didn't question the why of it until later. It was a given, like original sin, a belief she would have shared with the staff at the mission.

Born Grace Geraldine Howard in a fly-speck Texas panhandle town, Mom always went by 'Jerry'. She never spoke about her 1945 marriage to Bob Gamble that left her saddled with me and my younger sister. After the divorce Mom, Nancy and I moved in with Bob's parents in Missoula, while Bob took off with his new love for parts unknown.

Even the mention of Bob was too much for Mom, something I learned at five when I was kneeling for my bedtime prayer:

"Now I lay me down to sleep,
I pray to God my soul to keep
If I should die before I wake
I pray to God my soul to take. Amen"

I had easily mastered this rote prayer, though I didn't care for that third line, and withoutMom's encouragement, I began to extemporize.

"God bless Mommy and Nancy and Grandma and Grandpa and all the little children in China and Africa, and Bob and everybody in the whole world. Amen."

"We don't say his name in this house!" She hissed, her fingers scary tight on my arm. "You don't need him!" She was almost spitting – or crying – and I never made that mistake again.

In 1951, mom married Walter Dodd, a local rancher she met at church, and the three of us went to live with him and his parents, Al and Myrtle, on their ranch twelve miles outside town. Although we never went hungry, there was no electricity or telephone. It was a hardscrabble, subsistence life, and everyone worked, even Nancy and I.

I'd never had a permanent father and, biology aside; my mother promised me that Walter would be the real thing, whatever that was. I heard, but doubted. I was in school five days a week, and my personal time with Walter seemed nonexistent.

He roughhoused with the dogs but not with me and seldom played at anything. We didn't go to movies and I never saw him with a book. From what I could see, all he did was work. He started before I woke up and continued past my bedtime. He labored in barns, fields and pastures. He cared for animals, repaired machinery and performed scores of other tasks beyond my ken.

Most conversations were about the ranch: it was time to clean the chicken house; a section of fence needed new posts; the milk cows should be moved to fresh pasture. He never hit me and seldom raised his voice. He also never showed me much affection and seldom complimented me on anything.

Conversations with mom were like parachuting from a burning airplane: unavoidable but fraught with dangerous possibilities. According to her, my flaws could be arranged like the menu at a Chinese restaurant: argumentative from column 'A', belligerent from column 'B', and childish from column 'C' with a plethora of options left over. My defects were legion, and unless I got right with God, irreparable. Mom said so.

"It's right there in Proverbs, Douglas, 'Pride goeth before a fall.'"

At school, I was a good student though my teachers claimed I was angry for no apparent reason. I remember the day I came home with a new word – idiosyncrasies – and my feeling of superiority when neither of my parents recognized it. My anger and arrogance fed off each other and when they ran head on into my emotional insecurity, I exploded. No one knew what to do with me, and as I got older I couldn't wait to escape the ranch.

Chapter 5

Savage Summers

Summers of 1965 and 1966, Yellowstone Park

"Now Douglas, try to act like you've got good sense!" I'm not sure if she did it deliberately, but my mother always seemed to know just what to say to annoy me. I had finished my second year at Montana State University in Missoula where I'd majored in History and Political Science. I had continued to live and work on the ranch while my parents paid for everything - board and room, books, and tuition. It was a sweet deal and I hated it. I was nineteen, wise with the special stupidity of youth and eternally sick of working on the 3-D. Now I would be away from home, unsupervised, for an entire summer. Maybe she had a point.

Earlier that spring, I spotted a Yellowstone Park Company ad offering employment 'In the shadow of Old Faithful'. I applied, and as soon as school was out, fled the ranch. I spent the next three months bussing tables in the Camper's Cabins Café while I struggled to forget my mother's parting adage.

Yellowstone Park had its own language and rules. The tourists were all Dudes, and most employees were Savages like me: college kids, far from home, working a summer job in one of the world's unique places. First year employees weren't allowed personal vehicles, so to see the park we had to learn to 'thumb'. I caught dozens of rides that first summer and traveled hundreds of miles throughout the Park. I learned to pick a good traveling companion, preferably female, paste on a smile and wait.

Savages at Old Faithful lived in crude, dry cabins grouped around a communal washroom. The beds were old military style cots - nothing but narrow angle-iron frames, each one crosshatched with a network of horizontal, tentacle-like springs that sagged alarmingly. Their thin, lumpy mattresses were stuffed with what felt like pine cones but might have been straw. These miserable, procrustean devices emitted piercing shrieks and squeaks with every toss and turn of their unhappy occupant.

The best and most expensive place to stay in the park was the Old Faithful Inn. The Inn, a huge rustic yet luxurious log pile built in 1904, and renovated periodically ever since, was the largest log building in the world. A 500-ton stone fireplace dominated its open lobby, ringed by four levels of balconies that rose 92 feet to the gable ceiling.

The first Winnebago had yet to roll off the production line, and most tourists, the great unwashed, could not afford the Inn and so stayed in the Camper's Cabins ghetto, cheek by jowl with us Savages, as slum dwellers. You might expect there to be a fellowship of the oppressed, a sense of shared hardships to exist between Savages and Dudes living in the same miserable hovels. Instead, some guests seemed angry with us. They knew life was rough, seemed sure *They Deserved Better*, and resented the fact that we Savages appeared to revel in our miserable conditions. They were only partially correct. Some Savages, those obsessively attached to indoor plumbing or harboring phobias of large, carnivorous mammals had already quit during their first week. My years on the 3-D had made me immune to such minor inconveniences, so I returned to the park the following summer.

Pa Ed, Bob's father and my grandfather, had glaucoma and in the spring of 1966, when he could no longer drive, gave me his eleven-year-old Plymouth. Returning employees could bring their personal vehicles to the park, so although I was still painfully shy around girls, I became instantly popular. Nearly every week, four or six or as many of us as possible squeezed into my four-door, two-toned beauty and hit the road for West Yellowstone.

West Yellowstone, or simply West, was thirty miles away, just across the border into Montana. Perched in rather ordinary mountains at 6,600 feet above sea level, West featured genuine cowboy bars where drinks flowed freely and some bartenders weren't fussy about IDs.

Revolution was in the air and it was time to push boundaries. We didn't march against the war or sit in for civil rights, and we certainly didn't protest to preserve the environment. For many of us those movements came later, but that summer we rebelled against blind, complacent power and the park rangers were the perfect symbol of that humorless authority. In their drab uniforms they seemed rigid and obsessed with rules and signs. *No Parking. Speed 25 MPH. Do not feed the bears. No Hot Potting.* My heart leaps at the memory.

Performed correctly, hot potting was a nocturnal, co-educational sport, involving skinny-dipping in a creek or river. The key was to locate the areas where the almost boiling water from one of the park's geothermal springs entered the frigid river and created God's own Jacuzzi. As simple Savages, we made hot potting a rite of passage into our tribe despite the rangers' assertions that we were risking horrible burns, and 'damaging the algae'. Hot potting was a violation of federal law and, of course, a firing offense so we had to evade rather than just ignore the Rangers.

Although I was fired that summer, it wasn't for hot potting. It happened the day after I committed negligent bear-slaughter and it was really the bear's fault for jaywalking outside a crosswalk. The fiasco started the night before the Fourth of July, one of the Park's busiest days, when Lin and Suzie, two waitresses at the Inn, caught me as I headed for the showers after work.

Lin was out of my league as a girlfriend: blond and scary-beautiful, she hailed from Colorado and money. Her Barbie exterior hid a quick, fiendish sense of humor, and we both enjoyed impromptu-let's-pretend performances in front of other Savages. One of our favorite shticks involved Lin's mother, our dog Fang and our supposed marriage. Freud would have had a field day, but we didn't care. It was more fun than working.

"Hey Doug, whatcha got going? You want to head for West? We could take Fang." Lin flashed her cheerleader smile.

"I'm off till tomorrow at noon, so sure. But you know Fang drools – and the seats are still covered with hair from the last time."

"Don't talk like that, you'll hurt his feelings. You know how sensitive he is," Lin protested.

"You should of thought of that before you let your mom palm him off on us. I never would have married you if I'd known about that dog." I stuck out my lower lip.

"You two are total fruitcakes," Suzie put in. "Nobody would marry either of you goofs. Stop arguing about an invisible dog. I'll get Texas Mike and see if Dave and Dawn want to go."

Suzie returned with Mike, Dave and Dawn, and an extra couple I didn't know, and the eight of us hit the road for West. It was a grand evening. Nobody passed out, threw up, burst into tears or started a fight. Lin and I babbled like happy idiots and sometime between one and two a.m., the eight of us gathered at the Plymouth and headed home toward Old Faithful. I was the only completely sober person in the car. Texas Mike, with Suzie on his lap and an open beer in his hand, rode in front with Lin and me, while Dawn, Dave and the mystery couple held down the back seat.

Texas Mike may not have hailed from Texas, but he had a drawl and a big belt buckle so we took his origin on faith. A tall, rawboned kid, already working on a gut, Mike was a bellman at the Lodge and spent most of his off work hours partying. He was generous, puppy-friendly and always chipped in for gas on our road trips.

We were halfway home, no lights ahead or behind, when I came out of a curve doing about fifty and hit the gas. A piece of black moved into the road on the edge of my high beams, two tiny red dots gleamed and I slammed the brake pedal to the floor. The nose of the Plymouth dipped just before the black thing hit my bumper and rolled. Suzie screamed as she bounced between Mike and the dash, and we slid to a stop in the middle of the road, the engine dead.

"Yeehaw!" Mike popped his door and lurched out into the night. "We got us a bear!" He staggered to the front of the car and kicked at the twitching black lump lying in the road.

"Holy shit, Mike, be careful, it's still moving," I shouted, but to no avail. Mike stumbled and grabbed the hood for support, nearly falling on the bear in the process.

"Mike!" Suzie's banshee shriek was deafening, but effective. Mike jumped back. The bear shuddered a final time, and was still. Everyone climbed out of the car, chattering excitedly, and I assessed the damage. Steam rose from beneath the hood as leaking coolant met the chill night air. I cut the headlights. The sky was full of stars but with only parking lights, darkness pushed in from all sides and we huddled closer. The hot engine ticked as it cooled and the road stayed dark in both directions.

"Hey Doug, Dawn and I need to get home." I didn't know Dave very well, but up until then he'd seemed like a reasonable person.

"Yeah Dave, we all do. Unfortunately, it won't be in my car. Smokey here pushed the fan into the radiator. You could walk. We're only about eight or ten miles from the Lodge."

"Walk? But there're bears out there!"

"Well now there's one less. Look Dave, don't worry, somebody will be along. Right now we need to get this circus off the road." Together Dave and Texas Mike pushed the Plymouth onto the shoulder, but neither showed any inclination to lay hands on the dead bear. Mike gave the corpse a tentative prod with his foot and recoiled.

"Damn, Doug, this is like a gunny sack of Jell-O. I am not grabbing this nasty thing. What if it has worms or fleas or something?"

"Oh Mike, I'd worry more about wood ticks if I were you; they carry Rocky Mountain spotted fever. It can be fatal you know." Lin at least was back to normal.

"Spotted Fever? Lin, are you messing with me?"

"Gee willikers, Mikey, I'd never think of it," she smiled and batted both eyes.

I got my leather gloves from the trunk, grabbed onto a hind paw and hauled poor Smokey out of the road. Now it was time to wait.

Some minutes later, we saw lights to the north that resolved into a flowery VW bus containing a couple from California who happily accepted the challenge of cramming eight shivering Savages into their vehicle. We arrived in high spirits at Old Faithful just after 3am.

The rangers didn't even write me a ticket. With no useful witnesses, I guess they figured having my radiator destroyed by a black bear was punishment enough. Technically, the Yellowstone Park Company didn't fire me for hitting the bear either. Instead, management cited vague complaints by nameless Dudes of 'excessive noise' in the Savage housing area that same morning, and terminated me forthwith. Fortuitously, they also fired Lin, my alleged partner in crime. Our dismissal became an instant 'cause celebre' among the Savage population and a petition began circulating demanding our reinstatement. I still have a copy of the original, hand written document, with over eighty signatures, many penned by my once and future passengers. Tourist season was in full swing, restaurants were packed, rebellion was blowin' in the wind and management was nervous. Lin and I were re-hired the next day.

Besides my first firing, the summer also marked my first experience with drugs thanks to the help of Mimi Hargrove, my almost girlfriend. One afternoon in late July as I came off my shift at the café, she stepped out from behind a dumpster and beckoned. Mimi was beautiful, with long jet-black hair and a cool sophisticated air; I wondered what she saw in me.

"Hi Mimi, what's up?" She glanced around conspiratorially, took my arm and led me back into the trees. Bemused, I went willingly. "What is it?" I tried again.

"Not here! Let's walk over to the laundry." When we were well away from the café she began to whisper. "You know about grass, right?" I didn't answer right away and she persisted. "You know, weed, pot, marijuana?" I nodded dumbly.

"Yeah, sure I know," I finally blurted.

"Well, do you want to smoke some?" As usual in moments of social or moral crisis my mind went blank and my throat dry. "Well, do you?" Without conscious thought, I managed a nod and we were off.

While she led me over to the Dude's cabin area, Mimi explained that she had met a couple of 'actual hippies' and they had invited her to 'drop by to smoke a joint'. Mimi may have been a flirt but she was also cautious, so she accepted with the condition that she could bring her friend.

As life-changing events go, my introduction to drugs was disappointing. There was a small, dim cabin, two faceless long hairs, a smell like burning fall leaves and Bob Dylan playing in the background. During the actual smoking, I coughed a lot and my throat burned. After two joints, Mimi and I left and started walking back to the Savage cabins.

"It's so bright out here and I'm so stoned! Wasn't that cool music? What did you think?" Mimi chattered, taking my hand. I didn't feel very high, but didn't want to tell Mimi.

"Yeah, thanks for inviting me. I really liked that music. I've never heard anything like it. I'm really hungry; you want to get something to eat?" Mimi smiled and gave me a hug.

"So you got the munchies, huh? Me too and don't worry, it took me a couple of times before I could get a good high. You'll learn how to really hold your tokes and not cough." Off we went to the Camper's Cabins Café where we gorged on burgers with fries and milkshakes. That was my only experience with pot that summer and by itself unremarkable.

As August 1966 rushed to an end it seemed little had changed. I was not yet twenty-one years old, still didn't drink and despite some heavy petting with Mimi, remained a virgin. On the other hand, I had tried pot, and although I didn't know it, I would soon be a practiced toker and neither virginal nor sober.

CHAPTER 6

LEAVING HOME

1966 – 1967 MISSOULA

When I returned from Yellowstone in the fall I wanted a place where I could do as I pleased. If I wanted to drink, smoke pot and party – not that I necessarily would choose those things mind you – it would be my decision. I'd saved nearly $1,500 over the summer, enough, I hoped, for tuition, books and housing for about half a year. Just in case, I applied for a student loan and started a search for my dream apartment

After finding most places too expensive, I stumbled onto a pair of trolls who offered their unfinished basement lair, which they euphemistically referred to as 'a cozy, furnished studio with private entrance'. They were partially right. The entrance was a shrub-shrouded doorway so private as to be nearly invisible. Access was via the alley through a weed-choked backyard cut by a narrow meandering trail that seemed to be paved entirely with dog feces.

The room was definitely cozy. The ceiling – just the exposed floor joists for the main floor – was too low for me to stand erect, and the single room was stuffed with stove, refrigerator, table, chairs, bed and sofa. Next to the sofa crouched a washer and dryer, which I would share with the trolls.

Beyond 'cozy' and 'private' I can't think of any semi-positive adjectives. The bare concrete walls dripped water, and the lighting was dim at best. Then there was the furniture. The couch, a pied beauty that might have once been blue-ish, smelled like it had been marinated in cat urine and beer, coated with Karo syrup and sprinkled with dog hair. With its four broken springs it was like being embraced by a snaggletooth drunk.

Despite its lack of any discernable redeeming features, I was desperate. As I prepared to sign the lease, I met – or rather heard – the trolls' progeny.

"Ker-whump!" I flinched as a thunderous crash, inches from my head, reverberated throughout the basement. Before the echoes died, a staccato "Rat-a-tat-tat!" hammered my ears. Perhaps a tap-dancing elephant had knocked over the refrigerator?

"What was that?" I gasped involuntarily.

"Oh, that's just the twins, home from school." Mrs. Troll shouted over the din.

Unable to face one night, much less a semester among these bedlamites, I returned the unsigned lease to the trolls, fled to the ranch and tried to cope. Of course nothing had changed. Myrtle was still a tyrant and Al still slouched from meaningless chore to chore, the only evidence of his passing a haze of pipe smoke. Dad still worked like a machine, dawn to dusk, day after day, and Mom still didn't understand.

"I swan, Douglas, I don't know why you want a place in town when you have a perfectly good room right here," she informed me.

"Yeah, well I don't want to live 'right here', twelve miles from town at the end of the road. I want to spend time with my friends. I'm twenty-one and you still act like I'm fifteen." We had wasted years butting heads and a week after I returned to the ranch we were barely speaking. It was too late for something as mundane as family counseling. I endured Thanksgiving with gritted teeth and seethed with frustration.

Then, around the first of December, a laid-back guy in my International Relations seminar announced that he had rented an unfurnished house and needed a roommate. I approached him after class.

"My name's Doug and I've been looking for a place. Where is it and how much is the rent?" I asked.

"Call me Bieri. It's on Orange and Pine and it rents for $500 plus utilities so I figure about $300 apiece. Want to go take a look?"

Bieri and I hopped into his Rambler American sedan and tooled across town. On the way he fired up a joint and handed me the doobie without asking if I smoked. I took a deep hit and handed it back.

"Good shit," I gasped, doing my best not to gag. By the time we reached Bieri's place I nearly fell out of the car. The next day I gave him $300 and moved in.

Now that I had my own room, I could entertain guests – female guests if I wished – and I certainly did wish. I was still absurdly awkward around girls, but I had entered a world whose inhabitants seemed engaged in 'a never ending search for kicks'. In this new world, the women I met were equally comfortable lighting up a joint or initiating sex, sometimes simultaneously.

At first, I smoked pot mostly on weekends at the parties that materialized in our living room, but soon it was a daily routine. One thing led to another. If cannabis products were unavailable we fell back on alcohol or branched out to cough syrup with codeine, or nitrous oxide. A graduate assistant at the U's chemistry lab synthesized some DMT (Dimethyltryptamine, a plant-based psychedelic similar to LSD) which we sampled as well.

Drugs let me turn off my logical brain, ignore conservative Montana mores, and mock all of my parents' values: Get a haircut, get a job, salute the flag and go to church. Work hard and respect your elders. Marry a girl and spend the rest of your life with her.

Before the semester was over, I was starting every day with a joint, skipping boring classes, and hanging out with my friends in the Student Union where we scoffed at the PE and Business majors, and played chess, pinochle and bridge. One day during finals week in June, I was playing cards when Jerry Swenson, a grad student with some obscure, useless liberal arts degree, flapped over to our table like an enormous mutant Great Blue Heron. My god, was he really wearing a cape?

"Well hello, children! I simply cannot believe that you're just sitting here in a stoned stupor while I will soon head out on a road trip to fabulous 'Frisco where I plan to make a total spectacle of myself." Swenson, over six feet tall, reed thin and mostly teeth, had a shrill, sing-song delivery that drew stares from adjoining tables.

"Bullshit, Swenson, you don't have the nerve to go there," Joe, one of my opponents, sneered. "One of those old queens would drag you out of the closet and use you up in a week. We're trying to play here so if you don't mind just put a cork in it." Besides being loud, Joe fancied himself a wit and his partner Ted snorted appreciatively. Swenson's grin widened.

"Oh Joe, I love it when you talk dirty. I've got a space in the back seat just for you; it'll only cost you a share of the gas money. I'm sure you'd just love it down there." This last accompanied by much eye batting and leering. "Whatta you say, honey?"

"Hey, Swenson," I interjected, "that sounds cool, when're you leaving? I'd like to go."

"In just a couple weeks, Doug. You can have Joe's seat. He's gonna stay here, I guess."

Later, alone at the table, I collected the cards and reflected on San Francisco and the 'Summer of Love'. Word was out, and even in the Montana hinterlands, the eyes of hippies, anti-war activists, acidheads, free speech advocates and freaks of all stripes were on San Francisco. There, the music, sex and drugs seemed the perfect antidote to life in a society that in a year and a half had given us the Vietnam War and the assassinations of JFK and Malcom X.

After my last exam, I didn't bother to pick up my grades - I knew they were all 'C's, and a few days later I was gazing at redwoods from the back seat of Swenson's Ford as we wound our way down highway 101. It was really happening and nothing would ever be the same again.

CHAPTER 7

COOKING FOR JESUS

JANUARY 8, 1996 ` THE MISSION, YAKIMA

"Those boys on the Line don't deserve this. They wouldn't appreciate it no-how," Larry McHenry remarked to his wife Emma Lee, as he fingered the bag of gourmet coffee. It was Monday morning after breakfast and they were shopping. Three times a week, regular as clockwork, Larry, the big-bellied Texan in charge of the family shelter, would roam the kitchen and paw through the donated food for eggs, bacon, choice cuts of meat, and fancy pies. Larry never asked permission; after all, he was Staff and I was Program. Every staffer had a master key so they could prowl the kitchen at will. Nothing was safe from their predations.

As morning cook, I was responsible for breakfast and lunch seven days a week. Cooking at the Mission was donation dependent, so we didn't buy any food. If I needed something, I was told to pray for it. Even if God was interested in my shopping list, it seemed pointless to ask Him for specific items only to have them stolen by staffers. I hid boxes of eggs under a layer of chard or broccoli, and slipped bacon and butter into the darkest recesses of the walk-in freezer.

In theory, I had two cook's helpers and a dishwasher. In reality I had Robbie and a revolving door of the unwilling and the incompetent. It was easier to do things myself. Most days I spent eight to ten hours in the kitchen. I spent the rest of my time working on The Program.

We had bible study five mornings a week, and chapel before lunch and dinner every day. We had two Christian twelve step meetings a week. We each had to complete a series of Christian workbooks that parroted the Mission's fundamentalist theology.

The staff was held up to us as role models. William, our official addiction councilor, had completed a short course in 'Christian Recovery' and claimed to have once had a 'drinking problem' of his own.

"I used to like the beer, but I laid it on the Lord and He delivered me. Now I am completely free from the compulsion to sin," he crowed. William, who was about five foot four, and scaled out at over 300 pounds, had apparently neglected to ask the Lord to deliver him from gluttony, but then half the staff had weight problems. They might not drink, smoke or use drugs - they made an exception for caffeine, or as we called it, 'Christian Crank' – but food was a sacrament.

Overall, the staffers were not evil people, but I saw them as flaming hypocrites with no understanding of addiction. They regarded drug use as a 'besetting sin' instead of a disease and were always ready to respond with the applicable Bible verse or Mission rule. It was obvious from their condescending lectures that they felt superior to the men on the Line. In contrast, two staffers stood out for their humility, compassion and fairness.

Roy Brown, the Mission Chaplin, was an accordion-playing good old boy from Wyoming with a self-mocking sense of humor and a store of accordion jokes: "What's the difference between an accordion and an onion? Nobody cries when you cut up an accordion" and: "What do you call it when you throw an accordion into a dumpster and it lands squarely on top of a banjo? Perfect pitch." Roy had been a wild-ass rodeo cowboy on the way to drinking himself to death when he got religion and went to seminary. If Roy promised something, you could take it to the bank.

Ellery Banks' history was similar to mine. He had been an up-and-comer at a major local company when cocaine took him down. He had walked into the Mission broken, sick and homeless. He had turned his life around and apparently never looked back. As the men's program director, he was firm but compassionate and easy to talk to.

On January 24, I completed two months in the program. I was clean and sober, but financially I was standing on the Titanic. Besides my two maxed out credit cards, several unpaid fines and a thousand or so in other miscellaneous bills, I was in arrears on child support. The state of Oregon had set my child support payments at just over $1,100 a month so I now owed the state over thirty grand. In those first two months my only income, besides the $10/week stipend the Mission provided for program men, had come from sales to a local plasma bank.

Physically I wasn't much better. Institutional cooking can be very physical work with repeated heavy lifting and carrying. I had no reliable help, my back hurt all the time and I'd developed severe tendonitis in both elbows.

Emotionally I was a wreck. I was angry at the staff for what I saw as their hypocrisy. It was getting impossible to hide my contempt. The Mission taught that God hated all sin equally, but somehow my use of drugs was worse than their greed, condescending arrogance and pride.

If I could pick up an eight-ball and kick back for the weekend, I could ignore the pain in my elbows, and forget the forty or fifty thousand dollars I owed. I wanted a good, ear-ringing rush to wipe out my hopeless anger for a little while. Of course I knew that afterwards, when the eight-ball was gone, and my pipe was scraped clean, and I was crashing – I knew that then I would hate the mission, and myself, even more. Frustrated and discouraged, with no clue as to what to do, every day became a struggle to stay clean. Relapse seemed just a matter of time.

Chapter 8

Off to See the Wizard

June, 1967 – San Francisco

As the miles fell behind us on our scenic, nearly non-stop drive from Missoula to San Francisco, my anticipation became trepidation and finally, the morning we rolled across Golden Gate Bridge, stark fear. Everyone else in the car, Swenson and the two other passengers, whose names I have since forgotten, knew someone in this foreign place. A few minutes after we arrived, I stood on the corner of Haight and Ashbury, and watched Swenson's maroon Fairlane disappear into traffic. I never saw any of the three again.

I had no plan, no contacts and no clue as to how to proceed. What I did have, after paying Swenson for my share of the gas, was $320 and a powerful urge to get loaded. Two days later, I was sitting in a tree watching multicolored neon chicken wire pulse across the sky. Those intervening hours remain a maelstrom in my memory, but many events bob to the surface even today.

I remember walking all that first day among the motley crowds of mostly young, longhaired, brightly dressed freaks and smelling marijuana on the breeze. I remember later that afternoon, sitting on a stained mattress in a filthy, candle-lit crash pad, examining my sore feet. Around me a circle of sad, unwashed longhaired faces watched as Flash, a tall, vacant eyed, derby-clad boy, with a shirt like an American flag, and a pitch like a televangelist, shook me down for a 'donation'.

"Hey man, it's like this," Flash began. "It's groovy that you're here. It's all free and you can stay as long as you want. We share everything. Here, try some of this primo weed." He produced and ignited a fat, lumpy joint and passed it to me. I almost choked as the unmistakable tang of burning seeds seared my throat.

"Great shit, huh? It's Panama Red and you want to take it easy, it'll really knock you on your ass." He snatched back the stick of vile skunk weed and passed it toward a duo of girls who sat submissively on his left. They looked about 14 and the chubby one had a black eye. They both took puffs off the joint and sent it stinking around the circle.

"See, Dude, we share everything and if you need something we got, well, it's yours." Flash smiled expansively and gazed about the room. "Okay, we need to get together some bread for the community meal." He removed his hat, fished in his jeans and pulled out a tattered ten-dollar bill, flourished it for the group and ceremoniously placed it in the greasy derby, which he thrust at me.

I brought out a precious twenty, intending to exchange it for Flash's ten, but he grabbed it from my hand and, without a word, sent the derby hand to hand around the room. I noticed that no one else seemed to have any folding cash, though I could hear the clink of a few coins. Flash retrieved his derby and addressed the two girls still at his side.

"Okay, Moonbeam and Flower, you two go down to the Panhandle and see the Diggers; bring back stew for everybody." I never saw any stew and later learned that most days, at four or five p.m., the Diggers ladled out stew to any passerby for free.

The next morning I fled the crash pad and stumbled across a fast talking, sleight-of-hand artist who generously sold me a pound of what may have been oregano for $75. I remember, after that rip-off, following a hippie chick into a Brownstone and ascending a long, narrow stairway to a bright, high-ceilinged room where a stranger I somehow knew I could trust, sold me three hundred purple tabs of what he said was excellent LSD for seventy cents each.

Later that same day in Golden Gate Park, sitting in a tree, unable to speak, and peaking on acid, I watched as below me, throngs of hippies, dog-walkers, Frisbee throwers, picnickers, winos and assorted park denizens went about their daily lives. I don't know exactly why I was in the tree, but that first trip, when I saw the white light and the oneness of the universe, blew my mind.

The next morning, after a chilly night in the park, reality kicked me in the butt. I was alone in the City, hungry and nearly broke. I wanted to go home where I would find food, friends and the familiar. I considered my resources: the clothes on my body, a mostly empty wallet, a plastic bag containing 299 tiny purple pills, and my greatest asset, my thumb.

If two summers in Yellowstone had been my tutorial, this was my final exam. I found a spot on a main street and assumed the position: thumb out, smile stuck in place, and eyes seeking contact with the drivers. After about half an hour, a black Crown Vic sporting a whip antenna darted to the curb. The passenger window powered down revealing a muscular, balding guy sprawled behind the wheel.

"Hey, kid, where you headed?" He chewed at the words, the cigarette in the side of his mouth jiggling precariously.

"Uh, Montana, Sir."

"I don't know that street. What's it near?"

"No, Montana the state. I have to get home. It's real important."

"Jeeze, kid, that's way over a thousand miles and you're on the wrong road. Hop in. I'm goin' across the Bay an' I'll drop you off." I climbed in and was thrown back onto the thin upholstery, banging my head on the metal cage that separated the front from rear seats as he bulled his way back into the rushing stream of vehicles.

"You wanta hitch to Montana you better know the roads." The bulky Motorola mounted in the center of the dash squawked and spit gibberish but he appeared not to pay attention. "Look, kid, here's the deal." His eyes brushed over me as they flicked from road to mirror to road. "Hitchhiking is illegal in this state but if you stay off the freeways nobody'll bother ya. I gotta go up to the capital this morning so I'll drop you off on I-80 east. You gotta tell me something, though. What's the story with all these damn kids? I mean you're from Montana, for god's sake, why come to this fucking armpit of the world, you tell me that. I got a son about your age and he won't tell me shit. I mean you can talk, right?" He pinned me with his eyes and released a cloud of smoke.

"Uh, yes sir, I'll do my best. It's a little hard to explain but I'll try."

I described growing up on a remote ranch with no electricity, TV or friends my own age, where I worked for no pay. I complained about the boredom and bemoaned my distant father. Finally he could take no more.

"God damn, kid you got no idea how good you had it! No gangs, no drive-bys and your old man never beat your ass? I bet you even had a dog, didn't you?"

"Uh yeah, I did, his name was Pete and he was my best friend. We did everything together."

"You did, huh? Well I wanna hear about your dog. He musta been some special kind of mutt."

I found myself telling him Pete stories: about the time Pete started a stampede and chased our bull right through a newly built fence, or the time he disturbed a nest of bald-faced hornets while I was out berry picking and brought the angry swarm down on me. My benefactor lit another cigarette and eyed me speculatively.

"So kid, it sounds like your dog was always stirring up the shit, one way or another, that about right?" I dropped my eyes.

"He was a great dog, anything I wanted to do he was always ready. I uh, I buried him in the garden."

I fell silent, remembering that summer morning when I was fifteen and Pete couldn't stand up. Mom took him to the vet in town and when she came home a few hours later I ran to meet the van to hear the vet's diagnosis. Pete lay unmoving, a silent, already stiffening pile of fur. He felt almost weightless in my arms as I carried him to the garden. Jaw clinched and too angry to cry, I dug a hole. But as Pete disappeared beneath the black earth tears had leaked out of my eyes.

"Kid, growing up like that sounds about perfect, so I'm gonna ask you again, what brought you down to shitty, druggy San Francisco?" I had grown comfortable, but he was definitely a cop, so I didn't want to piss him off.

"You know about Karma, right?" I began. After his tentative nod I continued. "Well our society is unfair to like, blacks and poor people, and the war with all the bombing and shit going down. It's building up bad Karma for this whole country, and people don't even care just as long as they got their cold beer and ball game on TV and meanwhile we're napalming babies in Viet Nam. If you disagree, they call you a longhaired commie!" I'd been almost shouting. So much for not pissing him off. I had forgotten about the acid in my pocket and opened my big mouth. Maybe he would just dump me at the side of the road and not run me in. When he finally spoke he seemed sad, not angry.

"Listen kid, I'm a cop, I talk rough and you don't know me. We probably don't agree on much. I been around, spent a little time in Korea up at Frozen Chosin so I already know war is hell, and I'll admit I don't understand this war. It's like we're fighting so some tin-pot dictator and his old lady can keep screwing the peasants. But," he shook his finger at me, "a man's gotta do his duty, like it or not, otherwise, if people just obey the laws they agree with, you got nothing but anarchy! What then, kid? What then?"

"I don't know," I sighed. "I wish I did. My Dad was in the war, on Iwo Jima and some places I never heard of. He won't talk about it, but that was a different war. With Hitler and Pearl Harbor we didn't have a choice. What did the Viet Cong ever do to us?" We rolled along in silence till he finally spoke.

"Well kid, I asked and you answered, so I guess I got my money's worth. Hey, how long since you ate? If you're gonna hitch back to Shit Creek, Montana," he pushed out a grin, "then you better have some food. You ever eat at McDonalds?"

"Uh, I had a sandwich yesterday, but we don't have a McDonalds in Shit Creek."

He rumbled a laugh and flipped on his turn signal. A little later, after the best hamburger I'd ever eaten, I stood at an on-ramp to I- 80 East and watched the Crown Vic disappear into the cross traffic. My stomach was full; I had a baggie of LSD in my jeans and a sack of greasy fries in my jacket pocket. I stuck out a thumb, pasted on a smile, and waited for my next ride.

Chapter 9

Tripping

June 1967, the road, from 'Frisco to Zoo Town

Around noon, I caught the first of three or four rides that bore me from Sacramento, past Truckee, through Reno and finally dumped me at dusk in Winnemucca. I picked a spot under a street light, extended my thumb and began to fret. There was no traffic. My clothing was filthy and I was stuck in the desert 1,200 miles from home with a nearly empty billfold. I'd eaten nothing but a burger and fries for two days and, in case that wasn't enough, I was carrying a felonious quantity of illegal drugs.

Then things got worse. A silent, wild-eyed hitcher materialized and, limpet-like, attached himself to me. 'Scruffy', as I came to think of him, gave off a ripe, unwashed effluvium. His face and arms were mottled with bruises, and scraped knees poked out of his ripped jeans. I spent the night alternately sitting on the concrete curb or leaning against a power pole, as I struggled to remain awake.

In the morning two cars, a Volkswagen Beetle and an MG, pulled over simultaneously. The girl behind the wheel of the

Beetle was about my age, with a smile that covered her face. As I climbed in, I could see Scruffy pawing at the MG's door that opened miraculously to his hand.

"Wow, thanks so much, this is just outa sight, I've been out there all night," I managed to croak as she pulled back onto the highway.

"Oh, you're welcome. It'll be groovy to have somebody to talk to. I'm Sue and my fiancé Frodo is driving the other car. It's been a real drag. There's nothing on the radio but shit-kicker cowboy songs, and I hate those."

"Me too," I agreed. "I grew up hearing the stock report and the Sons of the Pioneers, and I don't know which was worse." Sue laughed. "So why are you guys in two cars?" I asked.

"My father gave us this VW as a pre-wedding present, but it was in Reno, so Frodo and I drove down from Moose to pick it up. That was cool, but this sucks." Sue stuck out her lower lip a tiny bit. "I want to drive over to Denver to meet Frodo's folks before I have to go back to work but it's too much hassle with both cars."

"That's a bummer, alright. I just want to get home to Montana. My ride split in San Francisco so I'm hitching. I was a Savage in Old Faithful, so I know Moose. Jenny Lake is really far out."

Over the next fifty miles Sue and I chattered like old friends and I was sorry when we reached Battle Mountain and stopped in front of a tiny restaurant. The MG pulled in behind us, the driver got out and came over. At barely five feet, hairy and kind-eyed, he could have sprung directly from Tolkien's imagination.

"Hi, I'm Frodo."

"Hi Frodo, good to meet you. My name's Doug. Thanks for the ride."

"Good to meet you, too. Come on, you guys." Frodo included Scruffy. "Let's get some breakfast."

Too embarrassed to cop to my meager funds, I followed Sue and Frodo into the almost empty restaurant as Scruffy trailed behind. As we settled in, a fortyish blond woman darted over with a coffee pot and a smile.

"Hi Kids, another day in paradise. You want coffee, right?" She began filling cups without waiting for a reply. Sue asked for orange juice and wheat toast. I ordered oatmeal, the cheapest breakfast on the menu. At $2.95, it was almost a third of my cash. Frodo ordered something called the Miner's Delight with double bacon. Scruffy clung to a cup of coffee and remained silent. Our waitress nodded and headed for the kitchen. Frodo turned to Sue.

"Okay, Suzy Creamcheese, what's the verdict?"

"It's a go, Frodo, if Doug has a driver's liscense." She turned to me. "You do, right?"

"Yeah." I pulled out my thin billfold and showed her my license. "I'm a good driver if you need a break."

"We need a little more than that," she responded. "See, Frodo and I want to go to Denver but we need to get the Bug to Moose. You're going to Missoula and Moose is on the way, so how about you drive the Bug to Moose, drop it off with a friend of mine, and then head for Montana? Can you do that?"

"You guys are blowing my mind. Of course I can, and uh, I kind of hate to ask this, but how do you know I really will?"

Frodo glanced at Sue and replied with a straight face.

"Doug, Sue can read auras and she's never wrong."

"Is that right Sue?" I was in shock at the enormity of their faith in me.

"Oh, Frodo is just being silly. I can't see auras. I trust you because, well, because you have long hair."

"Wow, I'm glad I outran those cowboys who wanted to shave my head!" I quipped. Everyone laughed, even Scruffy, who then shocked me by proving he could speak.

"Can I ride along as far as Salt Lake? I got a place there I can stay."

"Well sure, man. Just one problem, I don't think I've got enough bread for gas. Sorry."

"No problem." Frodo reached into his pocket. "We'll fill up here and you can take this for along the way." He handed me a crumpled twenty.

"Thanks, Frodo, but that's too much. Ten should be plenty."

"Take it, Doug, you'll need to eat too," Sue smiled. "And we really appreciate it."

When our orders arrived, the Miner's Delight proved to be a platter buried under a golden cheese omelet and a mound of hash browns, plus a second platter of bacon with a giant stack of pancakes. Frodo split this monument to gluttony between the platters and handed one to Scruffy. My oatmeal came in a huge bowl with milk, brown sugar, raisins, and butter on the side, and included thick toast.

A half hour later, our stomachs and gas tanks full, Sue and Scruffy switched vehicles and we said goodbye. I had the name of Sue's roommate in Moose. Life was good again. I got behind the wheel of the Bug and we were off.

Six hours later I dropped Scruffy in Salt Lake City. By noon the next day, I turned the Bug over to the roommate and found myself standing by the northbound lane of Hwy 26, with my thumb out - again

After about five minutes a purple Pontiac Bonneville with Montana plates came to a sliding dusty stop on the shoulder, beside me. The sole occupant, a flashy chick about my age, powered down the passenger window and, as her radio blasted rock music, waved me inside. With styled dirty-blond hair, clusters of beads, and rings on most fingers, she projected an air of unlimited self-confidence and I was immediately intimidated. This one looked like she might even have been a cheerleader. But a ride was a ride, and I was desperate.

"Uh, thanks a lot, I appreciate your stopping," I managed before I was slammed back in the seat as she hit the gas and, slinging gravel, shot onto the pavement.

"Where are you headed?" She looked at me, haughtily I thought, and as she switched the music from deafening to merely loud. I realized it came from a tape system, not the radio,

"Missoula, I hope. I started in San Francisco two days ago and I'm getting tired. My name's Doug." Not that you care, I thought, and why are you staring at me like that?

"Doug?" She exclaimed. "I remember you. I'm Claudine! We went to high school together. You were in debate or something, right? What were you doing in Frisco?" She lowered the music further and slowed to just over the speed limit.

"I rode down there with a guy and he split first thing. I hung around a couple days and decided I needed to go home. I guess I wasn't quite ready for the big city."

"So did you score any shit? Missoula's been dry for over a week. I was almost out of weed when a guy I know in Jackson calls, swears he has a good contact so I drive all the way down but the jive-ass punk is lying; he just wants to get in my pants. Really pisses me off, you know?"

"Sorry, I tried to score a key but it was a burn." I hesitated and then took the plunge. "Uh, I did pick up some acid, though." Claudine's eyes widened, her jaw dropped and she stared at me. I wished I'd kept my big mouth shut. She probably didn't do LSD. After a few more uncomfortable seconds, she started laughing.

"Well, well, well. Aren't you a surprise. You were always so straight in high school, I never would have guessed. You sure it's any good?"

"I'm pretty sure; I rushed all night on one hit." I smiled, remembering. "I really liked it."

"You liked it, did you?" Claudine chortled. "Okay, here's the plan. I've got a shit-load of great tunes, with drinks and snacks in the trunk. We drive right now to Jenny Lake, find a place to camp and each drop a hit. You cool with that, Doug?"

"For sure," I replied. "But I really need a shower. Maybe I can wash in the lake."

Claudine nodded, turned up the music and hit the gas.

Except for the initial rush, my second acid trip was completely different from the first. On my first trip, surrounded by strangers, everything took place in my head. In contrast, Claudine and I spent the evening and most of the night laughing and talking. I can't remember our words, but I felt at one – not just with funny, beautiful Claudine – but with the sky, the wind, the leaves, the whole world and even with the flying saucers we thought we watched throughout the night.

The next day, after a slightly awkward drive, we reached Missoula where Claudine pulled up in front of my apartment.

"Uh, thanks for everything, Claudine. I appreciate it. Let me give you a couple of these." I handed her a small paper bindle.

"Hey Doug, thanks, that was far out. We need to trip out again sometime soon, all right?"

"For sure. Catch you later."

Of course I didn't catch Claudine later, and the deck was stacked against our ever tripping together again, which was probably for the best. For the next several years I stayed stoned as much as possible, so I hardly noticed as my life spiraled out of control.

Fifty years after the fact, I wonder if that trip marked a tipping point. I had experimented with a variety of drugs and, like most of my friends, smoked pot nearly every day. Enmeshed in the drug/hippie sub-culture, we self-identified as 'heads' as opposed to 'straight people'. But what if those three hundred purple tabs of LSD had turned out to be a burn? Say sucrose and vitamin B, for example. Would that have mattered?

I was on track for law school and had already scored high enough on the entrance exam for acceptance at the U. in Missoula. Mom and Dad would have paid. Could I have stepped back from the abyss, gone on with my life? In theory, I could have stuck with marijuana and good scotch like some of my friends, slogged my way through three years of law school, and become an attorney, successful or otherwise. I'll never know, but I doubt it. I was already a deeply unhappy person; selfish and angry without knowing why. Speaking as someone who always learned things the hard way, I think my course was already set.

Chapter 10

Called to Serve

February, 1996 The Mission, Yakima

It was a gray afternoon in early February when Rick Phillips called me to his office. As I sat in the waiting room my thoughts churned. Did Rick know I was struggling to stay clean? Was there a problem in the kitchen? If it was the kitchen, where was Dennis? I hadn't seen him for over a week. Rick opened his door and I was relieved to see that Ellery was in the room with him.

"Come on in, Doug. Ellery and I have been doing some talking, and I decided it was time I got to know you better." Rick's dark suit emphasized his tall, thin frame and his black hair almost touched his collar. His slight smile was unreadable and as he spoke, his eyes remained fixed on my face as though, if he stared hard enough, he could look directly into my soul.

According to the other program men, Rick's father, Roger, a transplanted California contractor, had founded the Mission twenty-two years before in a dilapidated brick storefront on Yakima's main drag. Jammed between a low-end dive and a blind pig, the mission had been Roger's baby. Program gossip held that Roger had been carpenter and cook, janitor and preacher, and, when necessary, bouncer. He had apparently done it all, gradually gaining expertise and building support in the community, until, in the early 1990s, failing health had forced him to step aside for his son.

If Roger had been hands-on, Rick was a classic administrator, delegating the brooms and mops while concentrating on fundraising and slick brochures. The one time I'd met Roger, I'd seen a man without artifice or pretensions; a man who said what he meant and whose word was good. Rick was smooth as buttermilk and I distrusted him on principle.

"So, Doug, has the Lord revealed His plans for you?" Rick opened.

"Um, not exactly. I've just been, ah, waiting on Him, hoping something will come up."

"Patience is well and good, Doug, but the Bible tells us to 'seek' and to 'ask'. Have you been seeking and asking?" Rick allowed himself a frown that pinched his thin lips into a tight line.

"Well, I pray about that. Every day I ask Him to show me what to do and give me the strength to do it. But so far there's been no reply." I was careful to keep the sarcasm from my voice. In almost fifty-five years I'd never personally received a message from God, although I'd listened to plenty of speeches telling me about 'His will.' From Rick's fierce expression, I suspected I was about to hear another.

"Doug, the Lord has great plans for this Mission and He brought you here to be a part of them. Ellery and I want to move you into a trainee position. Are you ready, Doug?" Rick's voice had risen and his eyes blazed. Did he have special contact lenses, or what?

"Are you sure, Sir? I still have almost ten months to go to complete my first year."

"Those rules are guidelines. Your experience and education are unique among the Program men. Are you willing to answer His call? That's really the only question."

"In that case, of course," I responded.

"Good," Rick smiled. Now that the spiritual tap-dance was out of the way he was all business. "You'll start tomorrow as the Food Service Manager. Stop by Ellery's office, he'll explain the details. You have a great future here, Doug, thanks for coming in." Rick rose from his chair, grasped my hand and walked me out the door. A used car salesman couldn't have done it any better.

I walked across the courtyard with Ellery, still in shock. What did a food service manager do, and why me? Would I get paid? Most of all, where was Dennis?

"We want you to supervise the kitchen staff, provide daily oversight, coordinate food donations and plan special meals," Ellery said. He sounded like he was reading from a script.

"That sounds like a lot of work," I commented. "Will I get paid?"

"Not right away." Ellery didn't meet my eyes.

"Well when?" I let out a frustrated sigh.

"I don't know," Ellery sighed. "Look, Doug, I don't like this but…" His voice trailed off.

"All this sounds like what Dennis does? Am I taking his job?" I wasn't ready to drop this.

"More or less," Ellery admitted.

"So Dennis will help me with the transition."

"Dennis won't be involved. He's unavailable."

"What! Ellery, this is going to be hard enough. Without Dennis, it'll be nearly impossible. I can handle the kitchen but I don't know anything about the rest of it. I need to pick Dennis' brain." I was pleading now.

"Alright, Doug, you deserve to know. I hate gossip, but you'll find out anyway. Dennis is no longer with the Mission. He went to Vegas with a woman. Rick found out and confronted him. Rather than confess his sins and accept correction, Dennis chose to leave. It was a question of morality."

"Ellery, I don't want this job, especially for no pay. Dennis got paid. I need to send money to my family."

"Doug, I do understand. I'll tell Rick we need to pay you after ninety days probation."

That was it. Unable to resist a promotion, and the promise of some money, I started as Food Service Manager on February 10, 1996.

Chapter 11

The Lost Years

1968 to 1970 Missoula

My rough plan, when Claudine dropped me off in Missoula with slightly fewer than three-hundred purple tabs of LSD, was a simple one. I would keep a few tabs for myself, share some with close friends, and sell the rest for $3 or maybe even $5 each, tripling my money. As it happened I sold perhaps fifty tabs and, between myself and my friends, consumed the rest. Because I took acid over a hundred times in the next couple years, my memories of those years are unreliable. Some things I 'remember' may never have happened and I may have forgotten other actual events. Some things can be verified by outside sources. For example:

- June 1967 – Returned from San Francisco with LSD.
- February 1968 – Reported for draft physical; failed.
- May 1968 – Busted for possession of marijuana.
- June 1968 – Graduated University of Montana, BA in History/Political Science.

- Summer of 1968 – Worked for Northern Pacific Railroad.
- August 1968 – Plead guilty of possession of drugs and placed on probation.
- October 1968 – Met and impregnated Candy.
- June 1969 – Candy gave birth to a girl. I was not involved.
- Summer and fall 1969 – Worked for Bud Price
- August 1969 – Released from probation.

Some of my memories from these years are incredibly vivid and I am sure – almost – that they are real.

I remember dropping acid at my draft physical, and when the young Second Lieutenant asked why I didn't want to join the army, I remember laughing hysterically and replying:

"Hey, man, I could never be a part of any organization that napalms babies and, besides, when the revolution comes I want to be here to kill assholes like you!"

I remember opening my trailer door one night and facing a hatchet-faced cracker who would have looked right at home wearing a sheet and carrying a rope, instead of a badge and a smirk. "Hey Boy, you all are in a shitload of trouble," he taunted, and my heart sank.

I remember my mother's tirade two days later when I got out on bail. "Douglas, I'm just sick! Why, I'm so mad I could spit! The first thing you need to do is sell your stupid motorcycle, give us the money, cut your hair and move back to the ranch. Then we'll get you a lawyer."

I don't remember, but according to my diploma, I received a B.A. in history from the University of Montana on June 9, 1968.

Beginning August of 1968 I must have checked in with my PO every month, though I don't remember that either.

I barely remember my time with Candy at all, though I know a few things. I know she lived with her parents in Stevensville, twenty or so miles south of Missoula. I know she didn't have a car. She was quiet, had long straight brown hair and wore granny glasses and a long paisley-patterned dress. When I think of Candy I smell patchouli oil, and of that, I am certain.

I can't say why, but some of my clearer memories are of work. I remember working a summer on a steel gang for the Northern Pacific railroad. I remember one of the old timers on the crew, Shaunessy, a red faced Irish giant, declaiming, "We're Gandys, lad, and a good life it is. Work like hell all summer and when the season's over lay up in Portland for the winter. Portland is a grand place. It's got a fine skid row with plenty of flophouses. There's a passel of Missions; those Bible Thumpers are always good for a meal or a handout and it's dryer than Seattle. A man can do a lot worse, let me tell you."

I remember working for Bud Price, a rough, stove-up, ex-logger who owned a dump truck and a backhoe. Life on the 3-D had taught me how to use a shovel and to sweat. Until winter shut us down, Bud and I traveled throughout Montana digging ditches in places I don't remember, for faceless farmers and developers. Bud towed the hoe with his dump truck and I must have followed in his pickup, pulling his tiny camp trailer.

I think my job was to check the ditches for grade; but mostly I leaned on my shovel and watched Bud perform his magic. I also recall throwing together meals: bacon and eggs for breakfast, sandwiches for lunch, and random cans of whatever-Bud-had for supper. After, I'd step outside and smoke a quick joint. I'm sure Bud knew what was up, but he didn't seem to mind as long as I didn't get high during the day, which I never did. Sometimes in the evening, after a beer, he would talk. Most of his stories were about logging and they stuck in my head.

"I tell ya, Doug, don't ever work in the woods. It'll get you killed. I remember when old Bill Mercer got it. We were up the Blackfoot, hauling to Bonner and one fall morning, frost patches in the shade, Bill came barreling around a corner, hit a slick spot.

His truck went right down the bank, ass over teakettle, into the river. He never even got out of the cab." Bud's characters came with different names, but the punch lines were of a piece. "....the top log popped right off and nailed him, bigger than shit." or ".... that cable just about cut him in half." By mid-December, when we shut down and laid up for the winter in Missoula, the ground must have been covered with snow, but to be honest, I really don't remember.

Chapter 12

Sinner-man, where You Gonna Run To?

May, 1970 Missoula and Billings, Montana

Among the things I do remember, there is one vivid, pivotal episode I'd rather forget. I'd moved a few times since getting off probation and now shared a house with Dick Grant, a part-time dealer, and his old lady, Jean. Dick, an anti-war activist and Buddhist, had refused to even show up for his induction physical. Compared to him, I was just a stoned hippie.

I'd saved most of what Bud paid me, but it wouldn't last till summer when railroad work started, so I decided to go back to dealing part time. I knew a guy who knew a guy with some low grade hashish, so I bought a kilo. After I'd moved a few ounces, Missoula was flooded with a shipment of killer weed and my sales dropped to almost nothing.

"Hey, Dick, that super weed really hurt my sales. I've got almost a key left but no money for rent. The railroad won't start for a couple months and I don't know what to do."

"Yeah, I've got the same problem," Dick said. "I've got a couple pounds of weed I can't sell so I called a guy I know in Billings. He says things are really dry over there and he can move five pounds in a weekend, no problem."

A few days later, as we approached Billings, I was behind the wheel of Dick's girlfriend's red Falcon, carrying almost five pounds of cannabis.

"Hey, Dick, how do I find this place?" The sun was already low in the sky and I didn't know Billings, a town half again as large as Missoula.

"Relax, Doug, turn left at the next street. We're almost there." By then we were in a residential area on a bluff above a railroad yard. The blocks were large, each bisected by an alley. Dick pointed at a nondescript gray house.

"Pull over – I think this is it." The house was dark and Dick seemed a little uncertain, but I killed the engine and waited while he went to the door. He knocked for what felt like a long time and I stepped out of the car to stretch. As Dick trudged back to the Falcon, a cop car wheeled around the corner, nosed up to our front bumper and ejected a Mutt and Jeff team.

Jeff was fat and appeared at least fifty while Mutt, even with the handgun on his hip, looked like he'd come from a high school play. I wondered, based on their sudden arrival, if this was a chance encounter.

"Hello there, do you boys live here?" Jeff showed a mismatched set of yellow teeth in what he may have thought was a smile. If he was striving for kindly, avuncular, his sour breath and beady, close-set eyes ruined the effect.

"No, officer," I answered, "we're just looking for a friend but it looks like he's not home."

"So you're just hanging around, eh?" Mutt ignored my explanation and didn't even pretend courtesy. "Let's see some ID," he grated. A lit cigarette dangled from his lips as he thrust his hand almost in my face. I was reaching for my wallet when Dick spoke up, hands on hips.

"This is bullshit. You've got no reason to hassle us. We're minding our own business here. Why are you bugging us?"

"There was an incident and a witness saw a red car," Mutt blustered.

"That's stupid. There're red cars all over the place. You gonna stop every red car you see? You're just harassing us because we have long hair!" Dick was nose to nose with Mutt, who fingered his baton and glared.

"Everybody just calm down," Jeff interjected. "There was a robbery at a convenience store less than a mile from here about a half hour ago, and the clerk said that two white males about 25 years old fled in a red car. You boys, well, you got a red car and you're about the right age. We just need to see your driver's license and you can be on your way. Okay?" He showed his teeth again and I noticed that Mutt had released the snap on his holster.

"Alright, I get that. Besides, we don't have anything to hide," I said, handing him my driver's license. With a frown, Dick presented his ID as well and Jeff ambled back to the squad car to get on the radio while Mutt tried to look menacing. After a few minutes, Jeff returned and stopped in front of Dick.

"Richard Grant," he began, "you are under arrest for draft evasion...." Dick was moving before the word 'arrest'. Mutt made a clumsy grab and missed, almost falling in the process. Dick cleared the sidewalk, and, like the starship Enterprise, seemed to enter warp drive. He shot across the lawn into the space between two houses and disappeared, with Mutt in belated pursuit.

"Stop or I'll shoot!" Jeff shouted as he waddled after Mutt, leaving me standing in the street, stunned and alone.

I stood paralyzed in the growing dark, my thoughts flashing frantically from denial, to anger, to fear. The air had cooled and

I grabbed my coat from the front seat of the Ford. I had no idea what to do. I'd never run from the police and they still had my driver's license. I hadn't done anything yet, as far as the cops knew, but eventually they would search the car. I was still standing, frozen, when Jeff stumbled back, red-faced and panting. There was no sign of Dick or Mutt.

"Get in the back," Jeff gasped, reaching for the squad car door.

"But Officer, I didn't try to leave or anything," I responded.

"Yeah, and that'll go in your favor when you see the judge. Now get in!" Suddenly I was running across the street. "Stop! I will shoot you, you son of a bitch! Stop!"

I didn't stop and Jeff didn't shoot. I sprinted down the alley for a block and a half before glancing back to check for pursuit. Nothing. Jeff was undoubtedly on the radio calling in reinforcements. The area would be swarming with cops in a few minutes. I felt disoriented. All the cops had to do was cruise the streets and watch. As I stood panting, I noticed a lumpy pile of something underneath a large tree in the back yard of one of the houses. It was dark now, but I could see the ends of some planks protruding from beneath a canvas tarp. What the hell, at least I'd be out of sight and maybe they wouldn't expect me to go to ground so soon. I slipped silently into the yard and squirmed, feet first, underneath the tarp and onto the pile of lumber. The planks were stacked and there was a gap near the middle. I settled in as low as I could, tried to get comfortable, pulled down the edge of the tarp, and lay still.

Crouched on the lumber, I could hear the sounds of the street, the rumble of passing cars, the start of an engine, the slam of a door, the squeal of brakes and subsequent rev of an engine. The sirens were distant but, as I peered out through a hole in the tarp, I spotted the distinctive silhouette of a cop car as it crept silently through the alley.

I heard the barks of different dogs, the occasional mewl of a prowling cat and, now and then somewhere to my right, the whistle of a train. Voices crackled over two-way radios as the search progressed. Twice I watched a figure walk down the alley, flashlight beam probing the back yards, once falling directly on my tarp. Then things went quiet, perhaps for an hour. I was almost ready to move when suddenly, all too close, I heard a scratchy 'All units, we got one on the roof, 10th and Madison, respond.' An engine roared to life nearby and a patrol car raced down the alley, past my hiding place, heading in the direction Dick had fled.

I stayed put, and found myself bargaining absurdly with God. For the first time in over five years, I offered a prayer: "Lord, if you get me out of this one, I'll go to Portland and do whatever you want." After more waiting, I finally risked a look at my watch. It was after midnight and I had been in the lumber pile for four hours.

Slowly, quietly, carefully, I left my refuge and headed away from our original confrontation with Mutt and Jeff, toward the source of the train whistle I'd heard earlier. I lurked in shadows, dashed through intersections and hid every time I saw a car. After a few blocks, the street I was on sloped upward and I could see the railroad yard perhaps twenty feet below. That was where I needed to be, but my street was becoming a bridge and I could see no way down to the tracks. Far behind me, headlights approached. If they were from a police car, I was trapped. I had to get to the tracks. I climbed over the guardrail and hung by my arms from the narrow lip of the structure. My arms started to ache. As the car neared, my hands slipped and there was a moment of weightlessness before the earth rose up and smashed the air from my lungs.

As I lay in the weeds near the edge of the rail yard trying to breathe, I took a quick inventory. I hurt in many places but didn't seem to be bleeding. I decided to try walking and, although it hurt to move, the experiment was a success. A string of boxcars rolled by and I remembered Shaunessy's words the day he showed me how to hop a moving train.

"Sure, and that's a good way to lose a leg if you don't get it right." I skulked about the yard until I found an open boxcar on a long string heading west, and following his instructions, swung aboard.

Just before noon that day, my freight pulled into Helena, where I caught a bus to Missoula. I half expected the police to be waiting at the bus station but all was quiet. I called our apartment. When Jean answered her words came tumbling out.

"Doug, what happened to Dick? Is he okay? The police came by this morning looking for you but they wouldn't tell me anything. Where are you?"

"I'm back in town. The cops tried to grab Dick for draft evasion, we split on foot and I haven't seen Dick."

"Where's my car? How did you get back?"

"I'm sorry Jean, they got your car. I hopped a freight. Have you tried to call Dick's contact? We were parked in front of his house when the cops showed up."

"That jerk! I called him this morning right after the cops left and he acted like he didn't even know me. I think he's a narc! I hate him!"

"Crap Jean, I'm really sorry. I'm afraid Dick's in jail. He would have found a safe way to call you if he could. Listen, I'm really freaked and I need to crash. Please hang onto my stuff and when things settle down I'll come by. I gotta go. Bye."

I hung out for a few days in a friend's remote cabin and pondered my bargain with God. If I stayed in Montana, the police would eventually find me and I'd go to jail. Shaunessy had called Portland "A grand place". I had a cousin there who would probably put me up for a week. So, with no real plan, I snuck back to our apartment and knocked till Jean opened the door.

"Damn it, Doug, this really sucks," she raged. "Dick is in jail, the feds are going to prosecute, cops came by again yesterday looking for you and I have to walk to work. Oh, and the landlord wants me out of here, not that I could afford to stay anyway. I told Dick I didn't like his dealing, and now he's gone." Tears leaked from Jean's eyes as she slumped on the couch.

"Jean, I don't know what to say. I have to split town and I've only got enough for a bus ticket, but you can have my furniture, books and bike. Maybe you can sell them. The bike should be worth something. I'm gonna pack some clothes in this trunk and that's it. I'm really sorry."

A few hours later, I was on a bus to Portland. I would not see Missoula for five years, about the same length of time Dick would spend in prison. When I returned to the 3-D, it would be as a stranger. My home in the mountains was gone.

Chapter 13

Pants on Fire in Portland

1970 – 1973 Portland

In the America of the 1970s, before Big Brother and national computer data bases, a person in trouble with the law could still cross a couple state lines and make a new start. When I arrived in Portland all I had to do was lie. Clerks at the Oregon DMV, employers, landlords and even new acquaintances – I lied to them all. Fooling these people and institutions was easy and it convinced me of my own superiority. Now I just needed to become my lies.

Portland, only five hundred miles from the 3-D, felt like another planet. I had moved from dry to wet, rural to urban, provincial to sophisticated, and from white to multiracial. Standing outside the bus station, I was afraid people could smell the manure on my boots and see the hay seeds in my hair.

Over the past three years, I'd been using drugs a lot – pot and hash but also LSD. Now, in a new town with no job or money, I didn't know how to score. The realization left me strangely untroubled. I called my cousin and talked my way into a spot on his basement floor until I could 'get on my feet'.

Two days later I started work at Winter Products, a sweatshop where we took raw metal castings: hinges, drawer pulls, knobs and assorted doodads, and turned them into polished, richly colored, finished hardware ready to attach to fine oak cabinets, fancy birch armoires and antique maple dressers.

Winter Products could have been Satan's own creation. There in a poorly lit, unventilated, and windowless warehouse, packed with hot, noisy machines and open vats of toxic chemicals, I labored for $1.25 an hour.

My first paycheck bought me a month in a single room, bathroom down the hall, on the third floor of a chopped up Victorian monster in NW Portland. With my third check, I got a green 1951 Plymouth coupe for $100.

A few weeks later, a co-worker approached me in the parking lot.

"Hey, man, my name's Harvey. You get high?" I'd been clean over a month by then and although I was doing okay, my answer was automatic.

"Is a bear Catholic? I'm Doug. What you got?"

What Harvey had, besides great pot and a generous nature, was a powerful urge to mess up his head. Harvey's favorite drugs were marijuana and alcohol and he introduced me to several dealers and took me to dozens of Portland bars and taverns. I followed Harvey's lead and, for the time being, stuck with pot and booze.

Six months after we met, Harvey and I rented a house in N. E. Portland. Although we were still working at Winter Products, we both wanted to move on. In the fall of 1971, Harvey came to me with news that eventually made that possible.

"Hey Doug, a guy told me there's a laborers' exam for the City of Portland coming up. I'm going down tomorrow and fill out an application. You want to come along?"

"Sure! I'm really sick of acid burns. You know anything about the job?"

"Starting pay is $3.20 an hour, my buddy says the test is easy and they don't work you too hard. Comes with benefits too."

"Shit, Harvey, that's a no-brainer. I'm still only making $1.45 at the doorknob factory. Count me in."

Harvey's friend proved to be right about the test. We each scored 98 out of a possible 100, and, because of his veterans preference, the City hired Harvey almost immediately. I waited expectantly, but months passed without word from the City and I began to lose hope. Finally, over a year after the exam, I started work at the Portland Bureau of Water Works.

In the three years since I'd fled Montana, I'd had only minimal contact with my family. I called once or twice a year to let them know I was alive, but every time, Mom handed the phone to Dad after a few words. Time did not appear to be healing this wound.

CHAPTER 14

I WALK THE LINE

MAY 1, 1996 THE MISSION, YAKIMA

I lasted less than two months as the Mission's Food Service Manager. When Rick had singled me out in Bible study that March morning, my frustration had burst into anger and something inside me had snapped. The Mission was never going to pay me and I was never going to agree with their theology.

There were no written guidelines and with Dennis gone, I floundered. To the kitchen staff I was just a cook and their disrespect was palpable. I needed some help, and when Rick was too busy to even see me, I realized the job had been a sucker's bet from the get-go. I would always be a mission misfit, so why bother to try?

I had my own room and a key to the kitchen's back door. Miguel was still dealing and for the rest of March I got high regularly. I was still in the program and subject to drug testing but their schedule was predictable and for a while I dodged the tests. When I failed my first test that April my sincere protestations of injured innocence bought me some time. Now it was the first of May and I had another dirty UA. Ellery gave me an ultimatum.

"I don't want to lose you, Doug, but we can't ignore this. You need to re-start the program from day one."

"I've been working sixty or seventy hours a week, for five months, with no pay and now you guys, just to show your appreciation, are going to kick me out on the street. I know I screwed up, but if I have to start over, it'll be another year before I can get a real job. I have two kids, and every month the State of Oregon expects me to pay eleven hundred bucks child support. That comes to," I made a quick calculation, "over $13,000 a year. My annual program stipend is five hundred bucks. Ellery, I just can't do that."

"Doug," Ellery spoke softly, "you could have come to me when things got too hard for you, but you chose to pick up the pipe instead. I didn't say we were kicking you out of the Mission. If you decide to leave the program you can always go back on the Line."

I looked at Ellery thoughtfully. On the Line, my days would be my own. I could find a full time paying job. I would have no homework, no Bible study and no drug tests. Every afternoon I could sign up for a bed, attend chapel, eat dinner, shower and climb into a bunk. In the morning, I could eat breakfast and go to work. On Saturday the Mission distributed clean used clothing and offered haircuts. All these things were free. The Line had few other attractions, but I was sick to death of the program, its cult-like atmosphere and the work without pay.

"You're right, Ellery, I need to go back on the Line."

I moved back to the men's dorm that afternoon. On the Line I was expected to work for my bed each day, but as morning cook, I'd watched Line guys skate through their bed-work – bus a few dishes, wipe down a table or three and they were done. Ironically, since the Mission still suffered from a chronic shortage of cooks, as my bed-work I prepared breakfast as usual. Afterwards I fixed myself a sack lunch and went looking for a job. I enjoyed this arrangement and for a time ghosted unnoticed in the niche I'd carved out.

A month or so later Rick hired two food service professionals, a married couple, to whom he paid actual wages, for what he had expected me to do for free. Soon thereafter, someone informed the new managers that the morning cook really should be someone in the Program, not a Line guy, and they banished me from the kitchen.

Life in the fifty-six bed men's dorm was different, but I adjusted. The bunks were all two high and almost no one wanted a top bunk. I always preferred one. No drunks barfed on you in the night if you were in a top bunk. About half the Line guys were Mexican orchard workers and they taught me some practical Spanish. I learned that in the men's dorm, a shout of 'agua caliente', (literally 'hot water') meant 'jump out of the shower quick, someone just flushed the toilet'.

While I looked for full-time work, I picked up day jobs from local contractors and homeowners who regularly came to the Mission looking for cheap, temporary labor. The scene was right out of 'Bound for Glory'. A pickup would pull into the lot behind the Mission. The driver - nearly always a man - would carefully lock his doors and approach the lobby. The Line guys who clustered in the fenced yard behind the Mission, sharing lies and hand rolled cigarettes, would perk up and try to look employable. Some employers would negotiate with the men directly; others would inquire at the front desk. Many of the Line guys were quite particular. What was the job? What did it pay?

That was not my way. I never asked what a job was or what it paid, and I never turned work down. I was also prepared. I carried a small day pack (it was my pillow at night) containing a jacket, work gloves, water bottle, and a first aid kit. Most people treated me fairly, and my work for two of the families who hired me changed my life completely.

Chapter 15

Life at the Lazy W

1973 – 1974 Portland Water Bureau

> "Easy there, boy, leave some of that dirt for the rest of us." Big Wally

In Portland when I started at the Water Bureau, it felt like retirement. Nobody worked very hard and I did my best to fit in. Still, crew leaders said things like, 'slow down, take it easy,' and 'save some for later'. It wasn't like the ranch. There, when I stopped to catch my breath, Walter had asked if I planned to join the shovel leaners union.

Harvey had told me about the on-the-job drinking, but when, a little after noon my first Friday on the job, our service truck pulled into a tavern lot and parked, I was dumbfounded. Our crew leader, Big Wally, climbed out and waddled toward the door, followed by Haystack and Semi. Big Wally, barely topped 5' 5", but weighed in at over 250 pounds.

"Haystack," I hissed. "What's going on? What are we doing?"

"Lunch," Haystack responded, stretching his tee shirt over his bulging gut and pushing his curly, blonde, white-boy-afro away from his eyes. Haystack didn't seem too friendly so I turned to Semi, an older, hobbit-sized, crew-cut gent with a hearing aid and a vague smile.

"Semi, my lunch is in the truck. I'll just wait out here." By now my protestations had caught the attention of Big Wally who turned and fixed me with a porcine glare.

"Listen up, here's how we do things in my district. Friday after payday we kick back. You ain't been paid yet, so this one is on me. You understand?" He was not smiling.

"Yes, sir! I understand." I felt like a puppy, standing between a pit bull and a steak.

"Good! Now let's go." Big Wally flipped open the door and lumbered inside.

Before we could seat ourselves, the Amazon behind the bar had already filled a gigantic pitcher with draft beer. When she deposited the pitcher effortlessly on our table, along with four icy mugs, I noticed that her nametag read 'Bertha'.

"Hey, Wally, the usual for you guys, right?" Wally, watching Haystack fill the mugs, grunted in reply. Bertha glanced down at me. "How about you, honey, need a menu or do you know what you want?" She stood, arms folded, muscles bulging and toe tapping. Big Wally took command.

"Bring him an order of wings, Bert, my treat. We got us a newbie and I got to break him in right."

Wally hoisted a brimming mug and drank noisily. As he set it down half empty, I knew I was in trouble. By the time our hot, greasy wings arrived, I wasn't the only one. We were on our third pitcher and Haystack, who up to that point had matched Big Wally mug for mug, started for the men's room and instead fell out of his chair and hit the floor.

"Look out, Boy. If you can't run with the big dogs you better stay on the porch!" Wally laughed as he threw out a shovel-sized hand, hauled Haystack to his feet and shoved him toward the restrooms. "Hey, Bert, can we get another pitcher and some quarters over here? I need to give these boys some pool lessons."

As Big Wally inserted a quarter, dropped the balls and fumbled with the rack, I turned to Semi, who had been drinking quietly but steadily.

"Uh, Semi, that's an unusual name. What's it stand for?" I asked somewhat drunkenly.

"Oh, it's not my name. I'm John, John Hakenan. I'm a square-head. They just call me that because I'm semi-retired." He gave me a grin. "Wally'll find a name for you if you stay on this truck. Haystack's name is James, but he reminds Wally of 'Haystack Calhoun', the wrestler."

"So, Semi, do you guys always drink this much?"

"This ain't nothing. I remember when I started here in '54 and they put me on Frank Fague's truck. He was still in the field. Payday Friday, Frank pulled our truck right up to a Green Front."

"Who's Frank Fague?" I asked. I knew Oregon liquor stores were called 'green fronts' because of their color scheme, but I'd never heard of Frank Fague. Wally and Haystack were banging balls around the pool table so Semi and I were alone.

"You don't know much about the bureau, do you? Frank's the head of the whole damn division. Anyhoo, as I was tellin' ya, he came out with a fifth, drove up behind the Rose Garden, and parked. Frank opened that bottle and flipped the cap into the blackberries. We hit that jug till it was empty, and then Frank flung it into the bushes too." Semi paused and stared off into space.

"What happened when you got back to the shop? Weren't you guys drunk?" I prompted.

"Drunk," Semi scoffed, "on one bottle? We were lit up but we weren't drunk. Frank just drove back smooth as you please and you better believe nobody said anything about it." Semi belched loudly. "I can't drink that hard stuff like I used to." He rose and reeled to the restroom.

We spent the rest of the afternoon in the tavern, and while Wally and Haystack shot pool and gulped beer, I was treated to more stories of fearless Frank Fague, who Semi claimed, knew the burial sites of enough bodies to insulate him from all threats to his hegemony.

Just before quitting time Big Wally piloted the service truck back to the shop where I noticed that ours was not the only crew worse for wear. Still, none of the foremen appeared to notice. Frank's alcoholic attitude defined the culture of the Division and set the tone on Big Wally's truck. I did not fit in and was soon transferred.

Leon Hawkins was more to my liking as a crew leader. The Hawk was a rail thin, unschooled, red-faced Okie, and though he didn't care for long hairs, he and his driver, Clint Van Arsdahll, were fair, hardworking men.

The fourth crewman, James T. Jessie, or 'Jessie James as the Hawk referred to him, was one of the few black men at the bureau. Uneducated with a thick Mississippi accent, Jessie was built like a stump and a short one at that. In his late fifties with a bad knee, Jessie was still a good worker. After I came on the crew Jessie watched me silently for a few weeks. Finally, while I was digging for a leak in a 2" galvanized main, his curiosity overcame his reserve.

"Hey Dougie-Boy, Hawk tole me you done got one a dem 'versity dee-grees; dat so?"

"Yeah, Jessie, I got one." I punched the bar into the side of the hole where most of the water seemed to be coming from and levered out a rock half the size of my head.

"Huh. Doan seem t' be hep'in you much wit dat leak. Why you got dis job den, you havin' a edge-kashun an all?"

"I like to eat same as you, Jessie. Besides, I just love spending time with you and your brother Leon." Jessie laughed nervously, and then glanced up to be sure Leon was out of earshot.

"You crazy, Dougie. The Hawk he plant yo' ass rite in dis hole he hear you talk like dat."

I'm almost sure Jessie was wrong about the Hawk, but Leon *was* my greatest challenge, and in the beginning he barely acknowledged my presence. I resolved to show him I was not "one of them college educated idiots" he so disparaged. To do this I first had to learn to dig properly.

I'd used a pick and shovel a lot on the ranch but this was different. Leon expected me to dig fast, and produce a hole with smooth vertical sides, that was big enough to work in comfortably.

Leon was eventually satisfied but still not impressed.

As weeks turned to months, I noticed that when Leon was installing something in an excavation, Clint would usually squat at the edge and wait. Periodically, and without speaking or looking up, Leon would extend an arm and Clint would silently place a tool or fitting in his open hand. The service truck carried dozens of tools and hundreds of parts, so Clint was obviously anticipating Leon's needs. Usually, Clint would already be holding the next tool before Leon extended his hand. I wanted to be able to do that.

One day, while Clint was at the dentist, we were finishing the installation of a large meter assembly. Leon was in the hole, trying to tighten a bypass with an eighteen inch Stilson wrench. I could see he was struggling, so I picked up a twenty-four inch, made what I hoped was the proper adjustment, and held it extended toward him.

"Gimme a twenty-four," Leon snapped, before realizing what I had just thrust into his hand. I selected a socket and ratchet and waited. Leon finished tightening the bypass, held up the Stilson and we exchanged tools without a word. Relieved he didn't throw it back at me, I wiped off each tool as he finished with it, while scrambling to anticipate his next move. The rest of the job went smoothly. Of course the Hawk never acknowledged the change in our relationship, but things were easier between us after that.

I learned from Jessie James and Clint as well. We dug nearly all our holes by hand and one day Jessie was excavating for an eight-inch main. Jessie was five feet down and still digging.

"Get your ass out of that hole, Jessie, let Doug take a turn," Clint directed. Jessie threw out a few more shovels of dirt, set his shovel aside, and went to climb out of the hole. Jessie struggled mightily, but he was in too deep. The Hawk stood laughing as Clint and I, pulling for all we were worth, finally hauled Jessie out of the hole.

"Shit Jessie," Leon chortled, "I thought you knowed better. You start gettin' in too deep, the first thing you do is stop diggin'." That was good advice and I should have followed it.

Working for the Hawk taught me everything I needed to know about the physical work, but promotion in the City of Portland was by competitive written examination. My years of reading, memorization and test taking soon began to pay off, and when I finished third out of over a hundred applicants for driver, my future looked rosy indeed. All I had to do was not screw up too badly and put in my time until I could retire. Surely that wasn't too much to ask, was it?

Chapter 16

Time, Not Entirely Wasted

June, 1996 to February, 1997 the Mission, Yakima

"I need a guy for a couple hours to mow my lawn." The man was tall and a little stooped. He looked tired as he stood on the grass behind the Mission. It was almost four on a Sunday and I needed to be back for chapel by six. It would be close, but I'd had no work for days.

"My name's Doug," I stood up and hefted my pack, "and I'm ready to go."

"Kermit," he said. "My truck's over there." Although Kermit Jacobson and his wife Carol each looked to be over seventy, they both worked full time, Kermit at his vacuum cleaner shop and Carol in a doctor's office. By the time I finished their lawn it was past five-thirty.

"Do you have time to pull these weeds?" Kermit pointed at a weed-choked area in the corner of the yard behind the house.

"I'm sorry but services at the Mission start at six and if I'm not back I won't get to eat."

"I understand," Kermit said. "Jump in the truck." We were almost back when he spoke again.

"So, Doug, do you have a way to get around town?"

"I have an old Raleigh five-speed. It looks like crap but that way nobody wants to steal it. It gets me around just fine."

"Can you come over tomorrow afternoon and pull those weeds I showed you? Carol and I will at work. "

"Sure thing, Kermit, I can do that."

"Good. I'll get home about four-thirty so if you can hang around till then, Carol and I would like you to eat with us, alright?" We were pulling into the Mission and he handed me a twenty. "That's for the lawn."

"Okay, thanks. See you tomorrow." Kermit had known me for less than three hours, yet he was willing to trust a mission bum to come onto his property and work, alone and unsupervised, and then sit down to dinner. I managed to get out of his pickup without tearing up, but it was a near thing. I was ten minutes late for chapel but Roy Brown had the duty and let me slip in.

The next evening as I ate dinner with them Carol was full of questions. I shared some pictures of my children and Carol invited me for lunch many week-ends. My kids became a regular mealtime topic as I cared for the Jacobson's garden and yard. They treated me with respect and I never padded my hours or stole anything. Kermit liked to discuss history and philosophy. With only a high school education, he had decided to tackle the Great Books Program and I enjoyed our talks. Every so often Kermit would ask me about my long-term plans. When I had no answer, he would look at me with a sad, half-smile and change the subject. Although they liked me, they could see I was wasting my life.

At summer's end, when yard work began winding down, I started looking for a regular job. One of the other Line guys was working full time at Marc Packaging, a family company that assembled 'packaging machines'. The work was tedious, the pay was low and the employees labored in constant fear of the owner, Ted, a bullish overly tan egoist with a penchant for gold chains, white shoes, and polo shits embossed with tiny alligators.

The appearance of industry trumped actual productive work at Marc, and the company motto should have been "Look Busy!" To avoid Ted's red-faced, screaming tirades, workers had learned to always be doing something, even if it was actually counterproductive. Because he had stolen his company's best designs from Romeo, his dreamy older brother, Ted had no idea as to the actual workings of his own products. If he wandered by after we had just finished an assembly, and we had a few idle moments, we simply took apart whatever component we'd just completed. Ted never knew the difference; his ignorance if not our bliss, was at least our job security. I droned along through the winter, collecting my pitiful pay and spending nights in the noisy, crowded men's dorm. As long as I had earplugs, a book, and a top bunk, the dorm wasn't too bad.

Eventually, Ted somehow discovered that I had a college degree. Up to that point I had been just another employee, a poor working slob, inferior in every way to the great man and beneath his notice. Suddenly, I was in the spotlight. Ted took to watching me, as though puzzled as to what I might be up to, and his regard clearly was not benign. I was rotated through a succession of menial jobs - sweeping warehouses with a push broom, litter patrol on the sprawling plant compound in the biting winter wind, and cleaning out foul grease sumps with a shovel. In every case, Ted would drop by, light up a stogy and watch for a while. He would remark on some conspicuous facet of his financial success – his new, bright red, Dodge Viper, for example – mention that he'd barely graduated high school, and depart with a smirk. In February of 1997, Ted apparently tired of his game, and I was laid off.

Every other weekend while I worked for Ted, I took what remained of my pay after child-support, and called Miguel or one of my other contacts to score an eight-ball of cocaine. Then I holed up, usually in The Sunshine Motel, a no-tell dump on North First, and smoked away the weekend.

Some mornings after, alone and strung out, I wondered why I was alive. I barely enjoyed getting high but I didn't know what else to do. If I were to die, my children and ex-wife would get my pension from the Water Bureau. I was worth more to them dead than alive. Wrapped up in self-pity I was the embodiment of the Alcoholics Anonymous definition of insanity: repeating the same mistakes over and over, while wondering why I wasn't getting different results.

Chapter 17

Eruption and Extinction

1974 – 1980 Portland

On a Sunday night in June, 1974, a month after my promotion to driver at the Water Bureau, I got an emergency call from my sister that left me flummoxed.

"Hey Doug, you really need to get back here. Mom's got cancer." That was abrupt, especially for Nancy, who hated confrontation.

"What, since when? I talked to her a couple months ago and she said things were fine." I was stoned and not exactly tracking.

"No, you called her at Christmas and she's not fine. The doctors found a lump in March and she's already had a mastectomy and radiation treatments. They say its spread and she's starting chemo next week. Think you can manage to visit?" She slammed down the phone before I could untangle my tongue. I sat stupidly, her words reverberating in my head.

I convinced myself that after over four years the Montana cops would no longer be actively looking for me. If I was careful and obeyed the traffic laws I should be fine. Just in case,

I got a haircut. I made the 550 mile drive to the ranch on a Friday, paid my respects to Dad and tried to act like a dutiful, concerned son. Mom claimed to be glad to see me. Besides looking pale and weak, she seemed shrunken as though the disease, or perhaps the treatments, had sucked away the energy I remembered.

I left the ranch Sunday morning and drove non-stop to Portland. When I got home the yard was full of cars and before I opened the door I could hear the Grateful Dead. In the kitchen, Harvey was slumped over the table with a beer in hand and a zip-lock full of nickel-sized brown nubbins in front of him.

"Hey Man," he looked up and smiled glassily, "want some 'shrooms? I picked 'em myself down at the coast." He held out the bag. "They will fuck you up." Harvey was right; the mushrooms were excellent and I stayed up all night as the party gradually thinned out. By 7:30 the next morning I was ready to crash so I called in sick; after all, my mother had cancer.

The next few years were busy but not memorable. Off and on I had been dating Barb Woodson, an attractive blond I'd worked with at the door knob factory. Neither of us had been married before, and we decided it might be fun. It wasn't. Barb wanted to have kids. I didn't. Barb saw the glass as half full. I saw the world as a miserable place, run by idiots. Her happy nature clashed with my cynical worldview and after less than a year, we quietly divorced.

Early in 1977, I placed first on another civil service test and entered the city's three year apprenticeship program for Operating Engineer. I also picked up my first DUI but, since apprentices were not required to drive, I didn't tell my supervisor about my problem. I attended classes at night, and by day learned to install, operate and repair all the mechanical appurtenances of a large municipal water supply system. I soon tired of a job where the laziest men I had ever met spent more time playing horseshoes, drinking coffee and hiding from the boss than working, but I stuck it out.

On May 18, 1980, a huge explosion blew out the north side of Mount St. Helens and shattered the morning stillness with a boom heard sixty miles away. Within seconds, every living thing in the immediate blast zone was dead or dying.

I was thirty-four the day the mountain blew. Standing outside my Portland apartment that Sunday morning, I heard the explosion and watched the ash column ascend. Over the next week, the mountain seemed to dominate every aspect of our lives. On Sunday evening, one week after the eruption, I was home smoking pot when the phone rang.

"Hello?"

"Hi Doug." The familiar voice was soft, weary and slightly off.

"Nancy, is that you? What's going on?"

"Mom died this afternoon. The funeral is Wednesday. Can you get here?"

"I'll try. The roads through Washington are open now, but ash is still falling and the TV says to avoid driving. I'll have to go right through it." I didn't want to go but knew I had no choice.

"Dad needs everybody to be there. We can put you up at the ranch."

"I'll do my best. See you when I get there."

"Okay, bye."

By noon Tuesday I was almost to the Tri-Cities and well into the heart of the ash-fall. Like the sky, my mind was dark, filled with random thoughts blowing across the bleak, eerie landscape, and I imagined traversing the surface of the moon. The road unrolled before my headlights, a black ribbon on a field of gray. My speedometer hovered at seventy-five as I rushed reluctantly into the past, toward the ranch. Headed for the place and the people I hated and loved the most, my head overflowed with memories of Mom and my last visit.

After her diagnosis in 1974 she had suffered six years of futile surgery, chemotherapy and radiation. Her cancer had played hide and seek with the oncologists, disappearing from one area only to pop up elsewhere. By the end of 1979, her battered immune system had shut down and she had begun to work at dying in earnest.

Because Mom wanted to die at home, Nancy had moved back to the 3-D in January of 1980 to share the nursing duties with Dad. That March Mom after lapsed into a coma I had driven back to the ranch, but by the time I arrived she had rallied and confounded us again. I was preparing to return to Portland when Nancy told me Mom wanted to talk – alone.

Every conversation with Mom was difficult for us both. We had argued – some might say 'fought' – for as long as I could remember and since 1970, when I left Montana, nothing had changed. Mom was horrified and ashamed by my pot smoking, drinking, divorce and run-ins with the law. After the weather, our only safe subject for discussion was her cancer.

When I arrived Mom was lying on the couch. Dad had just given her a shot and her speech was slurred. As I sat beside her I could hear over the rasp of her breathing, the muted whisper of Butler Creek as it flowed over the small falls ten feet from the corner of the house.

"Douglas, I'm really worried. I'm afraid that when it's time to go I won't do a good job." Her body tensed with effort and her eyes bored into me. "What if I don't do it right?"

Gazing back into her eyes, I tried to understand. She was in so much agony, and had been for months, that death should be a welcome gift. I knew she was not afraid of dying. She believed, proclaimed really, sometimes with an annoying certainty, that after death she would be with her Savior. Her concern, as it had been all the years we'd argued, was with what people would think. Even as she lay dying, the opinions of 'people' mattered a great deal to her. If she died badly, whatever that meant, 'they' would judge her. Although I did not share her concern for those opinions, I squeezed her hand gently and tried to reassure her.

"It's okay Mom." I whispered. "You don't need to worry, not at all. When the time comes you'll do great. I know you will." Her eyes closed, her body relaxed and a small smile came over her face. It was the last time I saw her alive.

Mom's funeral at the First Baptist Church played to a packed house. I had smoked half a joint in preparation and so watched the proceedings, insulated and slightly detached. Dozens of mourners offered condolences and talked about my mother.

"Jerry was amazing. She was so kind, such a Godly woman. She put others' needs first." I didn't know this woman they exalted to the heavens. What had I missed? An angry wave of guilt broke over me and tears came to my eyes. Nancy noticed and came up to me.

"Hey Brother, you doing all right? I miss her too but she's with Jesus now so it's okay."

"Right, Sis. Everybody's telling me how great she was, like a saint, you know? With me it was always 'Stop that, Douglas, you know better than that.' I wish I could've met that person they're talking about." Nancy glanced around nervously.

"Doug, you need to get a grip. What will people think? This isn't the time to make a scene."

Of course Nancy was right. Mom hated scenes. I looked across the crowded room and saw, for only the second time I could remember, my birth father, Bob Gamble. Anything was better than the suffocating sympathy of Mom's best friends so I made my way over to where Bob was fidgeting and introduced myself.

"It's Bob, right? How about we get a little fresh air?" Bob nodded and followed me out of the fellowship center, down the hall past the minister's study and through a side door into the alley behind the church. He immediately fired up a cigarette and held out the pack to me.

"No thanks, man, I got my own, but I could use a light." I accepted Bob's lighter and fired up the second half of the joint I'd toked on earlier.

"What the hell?" Bob snatched back his lighter. "You're smoking that shit at your own mother's funeral? That's real tacky."

"You're the expert on tacky, aren't you? I heard how you asked Mom for a divorce with your girlfriend hanging on your arm. You shouldn't even be here." After that touching father-son reunion I stalked away and drove back to the ranch where I slept in my old attic room. The next morning, early, I said goodbye to Dad and Nancy and hit the road back to Portland.

Chapter 18

The Climbing Fool

1981-1982 Portland

The fall of 1981, Mike Parsons, one of the few good friends I'd made at the Water Bureau, asked me a question. "Hey, Doug, have you ever been mountain climbing?"

"When I was twelve or thirteen, our Baptist youth group leader led a bunch of boys up Squaw Peak, west of Missoula. We didn't have any equipment though, just tennis shoes and some walking sticks we picked up along the trail." I fell silent, lost in the memory. "It was summer but there were still some long snow patches. A couple of us sort of skied down those fingers of snow on our feet, standing up. I really liked that."

"You ever hear of the Mazamas?" At my head shake he continued. "It's a climbing club. They sponsor a basic climbing school every year." Mike slapped his belly. "Might help me get in shape and lose some of this gut. We could do it together." He looked at me expectantly.

"I guess. It might be a good idea if I found something to do besides get loaded."

Basic School didn't excite me. Still, the instructors were friendly and I enjoyed the conditioning hikes.

The next spring, on our graduation climb, we left Portland around midnight and drove to Timberline Lodge where we left our cars. We shouldered our packs and started hiking well before 3 a.m. As we slogged up the mountain I was at peace.

Periodically, our leader, Terry, called a halt so he and his wife Barbara could move through the group, asking, assessing and encouraging: "How you feeling? Is anybody cold? Try to drink some water. Okay get ready to move out." The students would shuffle about and then straggle back into line. Terry kicked steps up the switch-backed snow slope, while Barbara trailed the group.

A couple hours after sun rise, about 1,200 feet below the summit, Terry stopped in a small flattish area at the base of a sharp rise. The snow's surface was hard – almost like ice – and I was feeling strong and confident.

"Okay, crampon time!" Terry's voice rang out. "We'll rope up in a little bit but I want you all to get comfortable with your crampons first." I had fitted my crampons to my boots the day before and they went on easily. Several students were still fussing with their gear when Terry called out, "Okay, guys, you need to practice walking. It's easy to catch a crampon point and trip. We cannot have that when we're roped. One person's mistake affects everybody on the rope."

My feet were light as I walked away from the group, steady on the snow. I felt like dancing as I moved back and forth, drunk on the silence, the sun, and the clear air. Standing alone on the top of the world with endless possibilities, I wanted to be there forever.

"Have you ever used those before, Doug?" Terry's question broke the spell.

"Uh, no, but they feel great."

"Well, your ankles won't agree after five or six hours. You look pretty comfortable though."

"Yeah, these are fun!" I walked backwards a few steps, and then made a quick dash to the top of a hummock. "I feel like I could just run up that wall over there." I laughed with delight.

"I'll be darned! Hey, Barbara," Terry called, "looks like we got us a natural over here." He pointed to where I stood.

"Did you warn him?" Barbara smiled in my direction. "Be careful, mountaineering will take over your life."

"That'll be okay if it's like this. This is fantastic."

The rest of the climb did not disappoint. Each new experience was exhilarating and, by the time we summited, I was hooked. Back at our cars, I was exhausted but eager to climb again.

The next morning, I took my aching body off to the Water Bureau but my mind was still on the mountain. As I sat at my desk pretending to do paperwork, I realized I was not ready to climb on my own. Whether it was skill, equipment, or knowledge, I was lacking.

For the next couple months my climbing was limited to official Mazama Climbs. The club had a roster of trained leaders who organized and led climbs of various mountains. Each leader decided who could go on one of 'their' climbs and accepted new climbers like me only on beginning climbs. Those groups moved too slowly, the terrain was too easy, and I quickly grew bored.

I felt drawn from the city to the high places, where the sun burned on the snow, the wind was the only sound, and I existed wholly in the 'now'. I needed an experienced climber as a mentor. My chance came one afternoon when my phone rang.

"Hey Doug, it's Arthur. You have any plans for tomorrow?" Arthur was also a beginning climber and although I didn't know him well he seemed cool, so I was interested.

"Nothing special, Art. What's up?"

"My girlfriend, Cloudy, called. She lives in the Gorge, and she's working on her mom's roof tomorrow. She said that if I could get another guy – that'd be you – to give her a little help she'd teach us to rock climb. How about it?"

"You got a deal. Pick me up early. It's supposed to be ninety tomorrow."

The next day "a little help with her mom's roof" turned out to be the complete removal of two layers of asphalt shingles from a sprawling ranch style house under the blazing August sun. Cloudy, about my size but a few years younger, cleared away the debris as we hurled it off the roof, and kept us well supplied with water and helpful comments.

"Isn't this fun? I'm sure it can't be over 130 degrees up there," she said, as she tossed me another liter of water. I caught the bottle, wiped the sweat out of my eyes and looked down at her where she stood, face streaked with tar and hair sprinkled with bits of shingle.

"You remind me of what Abraham Lincoln said when a reporter asked him how it felt to be president. He said 'I feel like the man who was tarred and feathered, then run out of town on a rail; if it wasn't for the honor, I'd just as soon walk.' That's how I feel about this roof." I took a long pull on the bottle and handed it to Arthur where he sat, slumped against the chimney.

"Yeah, it may be hot, dirty and miserable, but that's the way us mountain climbers like it," Cloudy responded. Her deadpan delivery and bedraggled appearance were so incongruous I started to laugh.

"Well, if that's your idea of fun I can hardly wait for our climbing lesson." I stretched my aching back and returned to work.

Eventually the roof was stripped down to the plywood sheeting and our part of the job was done. Arthur and I left with Cloudy's promise that next weekend she would teach us to rock climb. It had been a hard day, but no worse than others I'd put in. Working with Cloudy reminded me of the 3-D and blazing hot days in the hayfields. She was, I thought, a person who knew how to work.

Next Saturday morning Cloudy met us as promised at a rest area east of Portland. As we climbed into her car, a hideous orange Gremlin hatchback, I noticed that the rear compartment contained what looked like the remnants from a climbing equipment store that had been struck by a meteorite. There were ropes, nylon slings in various colors and lengths, dozens of carabineers, climbing helmets and a pile of metal pieces that resembled nuts and bolts. I had wanted to learn to climb in the worst way and it appeared I was about to get my wish.

HorseThiefButte, just east ofThe Dalles on theWashington side of the Columbia River, formed a labyrinth of crumbling basalt outcrops, pinnacles, and ridges. I was skeptical as to how much Cloudy could teach us on the jumbled rocks and when she stopped in a flat, sandy area between two 20-foot boulders, I couldn't contain myself.

"What the hell can we learn about climbing here?"

"I don't know," she smiled, "that will all depend on you."

During the next four hours Arthur and I learned many things, including some humility. I learned to belay, set protection, prussic and rappel. I learned how to stem, lie-back and mantle – moves I probably should have picked up in basic school, but hadn't.

Two sandwiches and a liter and a half of water later, I was ready for more. Arthur, however, was not. With our formal climbing lesson over, Cloudy offered to show us some bouldering problems. Bouldering – climbing without ropes or hardware on low-level rocks was something rock climbers did for practice. Cloudy made it look like play, and I liked that.

By mid-afternoon Arthur declared that he was done so we headed back. We were walking, overlooking the river, when I felt a stab of pain, looked down and saw a yellow-jacket on the back of my wrist.

"Shit!" I jerked my hand reflexively. "I used to be allergic to yellow-jackets. I had a systemic reaction one time, my throat swelled shut. I almost died." My skin was red and I was trying not to panic.

"Don't worry. I've got just the thing right here." Cloudy delved into her pack and pulled out a battered gray metal box. "Here it is," she pronounced, opening a bottle and dumping a dab of white powder into her palm. "Now for the catalyst." Smiling like a mad alchemist, she spat in her hand and mixed the powder and saliva into a paste which she applied to the bump on my wrist.

"There! Now take a drink of water and you're all better." As time passed, I seemed to be okay and my near panic gradually abated.

An hour later, back at the rest area Cloudy stepped up to me and examined my wrist.

"So how's your sting? Baking soda really does work you know," she said, looking directly into my eyes.

We were standing close together and she had hold of my hand. Was it fate or pheromones? I'll never know, but without thought I leaned forward and gave her a soft kiss on the lips. Her eyes widened and she looked past me at Arthur.

"I hope we can do this again," I said. Then I blushed, hopped in my car and drove away.

Chapter 19

Get a Job!

March 1997, the Mission Yakima

Jobs in Yakima were scarce in winter, so after I was laid off from Marc Packaging I applied for unemployment and spent more time at the mission. I soon noticed that Travis, the morning cook who I had replaced, was on the Line now and always seemed to have a little money.

On most weekday mornings, a battered, extended-cab pickup with faded black lettering on the doors pulled up in back of the Mission. Travis climbed in and the truck left. Six or eight hours later, the truck returned and Travis got out. The truck was fitted with a pair of fifty gallon fuel tanks, rigged out with hoses and nozzles, and usually carried a chain saw or two in the bed behind the tanks. Curious, I approached Travis.

"What's up with the truck, man?"

"What truck?" Travis kept his eyes fixed on the book in front of him. He looked like a frat-boy jock and, based on what I'd seen in Bible study, a poor reader, so I was suspicious of the book.

"The dark green crummy that comes here twice a day, first to pick you up and then to bring you back; the one with 'Wolff's Wood Work' on the side. That truck."

"Oh, that's just some old German guy I help out sometimes. He's kind of an asshole."

"So it's a job, right?"

"U-hum." Travis was disinterest personified.

"If he ever needs another guy for anything, I'm available."

"Look, Dodd," Travis sneered, finally treating me to a glare, "the pay is shit, and you couldn't handle the work. Just forget it, shut up, and leave me alone."

I shut up, but I didn't forget it, and one Monday morning, when the green pickup pulled in, Travis was nowhere to be seen. When the driver's door opened, I was waiting with my back-pack.

"Travis didn't stay in the dorm last night," I announced to the barrel that rolled from the cab. "I'm ready to go if you need somebody to work." The barrel pivoted slowly and I felt myself measured by two dark eyes.

"It's tough work. Sure you can handle it?"

"I can out-work Travis all day. I don't take smoke breaks either." I spoke with false confidence. Travis was bigger, stronger and younger than I was and I was doubtful.

"I told the little shitter we needed him today." He twitched his head toward the passenger door and levered himself back into the cab.

"Name's Dick Wolff," the barrel spoke. Up close, he was below my height but twice as wide.

"Doug." I held out my hand and encountered a pair of vise grips inside a leather glove. I squeezed back, hard, and earned a raised eyebrow. I rode with my mouth shut as Dick rolled North on First Street, turned right onto the freeway and headed for Moxie, one of the numerous, little burgs that pimpled the Yakima Valley area.

"Ever split any firewood?" The question came out of nowhere.

"Sure. Montana first, then Oregon. Wood heat growing up."

"Well, I guarantee you never seen anything like what you'll see today. You pack a lunch?"

"I got some food and water, I'll be fine."

Dick grunted as he turned off the paved road and bounced down a long gravel driveway. He parked opposite a faded log house next to a cluttered wood yard. Canada thistles and Mullen weeds stood sentinel among the hundreds of fir logs loosely stacked in the northern portion of the yard. Random piles of apple and cherry rounds filled gaps throughout the yard. In the center of this chaos sprawled a wood splitter sprung from the brain of Rube Goldberg.

The splitter operation required two conveyors, a Case backhoe, two stationary gasoline engines and three humans. The work was noisy, hard and dangerous. Dick's son Greg set a brutal pace and didn't say much except to shout, "Watch it, Doug," now and then. When Dick climbed down from the Case at around three, I still had all my fingers. Greg just threw me a hard look and shook his head. I figured he didn't like me and that somehow I hadn't measured up.

"It's Busch time, boys," Dick ordered. "Doug, grab that cooler in the back of my pickup," Dick ordered as he eased down stiffly from the Case and hobbled to a seat on a huge cherry round. While Greg shut down the stationary engines, I carried the cooler over to Dick who pulled out a six-pack of Busch beer and divided the cans among us.

"Let's see, that's six cord, six hours, six cans and six dollars." Dick drained his first can and popped a second. "That comes to $36." He looked at me expectantly.

"Well it's better than a poke in the eye with a sharp stick. I'm glad to have the work and," I saluted him with the can, "the beer."

"Greg, you want to run him back to the Mission? Nettie's waiting for me inside. It's almost time for Oprah." Dick limped over to the truck and paused. "I'll be by around 7:30 tomorrow, okay? We've got another project scheduled."

Greg was quiet on the drive back to the Mission and I sat, uncomfortable in the silence. As we pulled into the lot he surprised me.

"You did okay today, Doug, but you had a couple close calls. Don't take so many chances. I can't trim fingernails with that splitter and it's not worth going to the hospital."

"I really need the work. I can't tell what your dad is thinking. I'm afraid he might want Travis back instead of me." Greg looked at me and laughed.

"Don't worry about Travis. He was always a pain in the ass. Ran his mouth all the time. You did just as good as him today and you'll get faster. Six cords is okay. Oh, if you have a long sleeve shirt you better wear it tomorrow."

Travis was waiting in the day room when I walked in, and even before he spoke the look on his red face told me he had watched me get out of Greg's truck.

"What the hell, Dodd, you trying to steal my job?"

"Dick came by this morning looking for you, but you weren't here. You didn't stay here last night. You were out getting fucked-up, Travis, so you did this to yourself."

"Ah, it's a shit job anyhow and the old kraut will cheat you on the hours. You two deserve each other, you little punk. Besides, I was gonna quit anyway. I leave next week for Alaska. I got a real job as a deckhand on a crab boat." Travis strutted away, having salvaged his pride.

I slept like a dead man that night and was barely able to fall out of my bunk in the morning, but when Dick's green pickup pulled in at 7:30 I was standing outside the Mission.

Chapter 20

Raised by Wolffs

1997 Yakima

"You ever been around a wood chipper?" Dick asked the next morning. We were ten minutes out from the Mission, and his question broke a long silence.

"Not really. Passed one on the side of the road."

"We'll fix that today. We're taking down a couple of maples and you'll get to know the chipper real good. Good thing you got long sleeves."

Dick was right. By the end of my second day with the Wolffs I felt and looked like I'd been in a brawl with a couple of psychotic beaver. My arms were covered with bruises, welts and scratches. My ears still rang and I had sawdust in both eyes. I'd also picked up a fat lip, all courtesy of Dick's wood chipper, and all par for the course. Without my long sleeve shirt and the hard hat, leather gloves, safety glasses and ear plugs that Dick provided, I would have been in worse shape.

If I'd risked losing a couple fingers to the splitter, that was chump change compared to the chipper. An old Vermeer, it could jerk a twenty foot limb from my grasp, batter me with it as it whipped by, and eject the limb as a blast of chips – all in the space of a few seconds. The chipper could just as easily swallow a hand or even an arm. I remembered Bud Price, the old ex-logger I'd worked for in Montana, and his stories of mayhem and death.

Dick and Greg got their day help from the Mission and, on larger jobs might hire two or three guys. Travis had lasted an entire month, but most Mission hires would start fast, full of brag and boast, only to burn out after a couple hours or a day. I got stronger and more accustomed to the work, and by the time summer came I was jogging from brush pile to chipper dragging as many limbs and branches as possible. Even Greg acknowledged my hard work.

"Damn it, Doug, slow down. You're makin' me tired watching you." Greg was smiling, and I was elated. He had remained aloof, waiting, I guess, for me to quit or just not show up like all the other Mission bums.

"I could use a nap and a beer but," I pointed to a tangle of limbs on the ground, "somebody's got to clean up your mess."

"I just don't want you to get blood on the equipment; it's the shits to clean."

"Heck, Greg, there're lots of guys who could outwork me, but there aren't any that actually do except you – sometimes." I grinned and trotted back to work.

One June afternoon Dick took me aside. "I got us a job poplar logging all next week in the Tri-Cities. We'll take the bucket truck, the backhoe, the Kenworth and the motor home. You want to go?"

I needed the money and Dick was giving me a choice. It was eighty five miles to the Tri-Cities and he knew I didn't have a driver's license. Glued to the dash of Dick's pickup was a plastic icon of three monkeys – hear no evil, speak no evil and see no evil.

"Sure. You want me to drive the bucket truck?" Dick nodded, and after that I drove regularly.

Lombardy poplars are large stately trees, commonly used for orchard windbreaks. However in an established orchard, poplars become a nuisance. They steal water and nutrients from the fruit trees and create unwanted shade. Dick had me doing the very work Bud had warned me not to pursue – and I loved it. That job turned into a half dozen more and by the time we finished it was August and I'd lost count of how many thousand poplars had gone down before our saws.

Back in Yakima my life returned to normal. Most days we took down a tree or two and I fed the chipper. Other days I worked around Dick's place spraying weeds or reducing logs to rounds. At quitting time, he would usually invite me into the house for a beer where I would sit with Dick and his wife Nettie, and watch Oprah. Dick would shake his head and laugh, bemused by this wealthy, articulate, Black woman. During the commercials, Nettie politely grilled me. Where did I grow up? How were my folks? Did I have any kids? Something must have met with her conditional approval, because a week later Dick made an offer.

"Labor Day is coming up. You got any plans?" I still lived at the Mission, and Dick was driving me back after another hot, dirty day. As usual, each of us had an open can of beer.

"Nah, with everything shut down, I guess I'll just take it easy."

"We're gonna knock off at noon tomorrow and drive up to Round Butte with the family. We won't start up again till Tuesday. Some yahoos been snooping around the house and I'm a tad nervous about all the saws and stuff. You could camp out there in Greg's motor home, keep an eye on things, feed the dog, and drink a little beer. How's that sound?"

"Heck, Dick, I'd be proud to drink your beer." I toasted him and crushed my can. "I'll keep a close eye on things."

I spent a peaceful three days in Greg's Winnebago, reading, drinking a little beer and watering Nettie's flowers. Dick's dog, Lady, was well used to me by now and I'd spent so much time around the place that it was the closest thing I had to a home. First Kermit and Carol, and now the Wolffs, had trusted me with their property. Considering that they knew my addiction history, it was an amazing gift and I was grateful.

Chapter 21

Avalanche!

1982 – 1987 Portland and the Columbia Gorge

I can't speak for Cloudy, but back when we first met, I was moonstruck. I was so smitten that I even stopped doing drugs, except for weed, something we enjoyed together. Two weeks after our first kiss we were living together in her primitive cabin on her twenty acres in the Columbia Gorge. My years on the 3-D had prepared me for candles, kerosene lamps and an outhouse, and though neither of us wanted to live that way forever, we were happy.

Late that summer and into fall, while we climbed as many mountains as possible, we talked of marriage and children. Things went well and on April 2, 1983, we got married atop Monkey Face, a freestanding 185 foot pinnacle in central Oregon.

I still had a few minor issues - some might say problems - but none I couldn't handle. I had quit drinking and was going to a few A.A. meetings. I still smoked pot on weekends, but Cloudy was pregnant and I was thinking about quitting. We traded Cloudy's ancient, Gremlin for a new Mazda pickup, and on November 27, 1983, our daughter Tiffany was born.

The next fall we started work on a new log house, one that would have electricity and running water. By May of 1985, the log walls were up. By September, the roof was sheeted and shingled, the windows and doors were in place, and we were camping in the construction zone.

I had been promoted again at the Water Bureau, from foreman to supervisor. I'd been at the Bureau for almost twelve years. In just eight more, I could retire with a full pension. All was going according to plan.

Instead of following the plan, I followed drugs. Ten years before, in 1975, I had gone to a party with my roommate, Harvey, and around midnight, when I was ready to leave, gone looking for him. Harvey was in the basement sitting on a mattress next to a coffee table cluttered with overflowing ashtrays and empty beer bottles. He clutched a small zip-lock bag holding two or three irregular, pea-sized, white rocks.

"You need to try this, Doug, it's a real rush." Harvey placed one of the rocks in a clear glass pipe and held it out to me.

"What is it? If that's coke I've smoked it in a joint before and, nothing – it's just a waste."

"This is different, man, it's called free-basing. You have to cook the coke first and then smoke it. You get an instant rush. Here, take a hit." He handed me the pipe and held a butane lighter to the bowl while I drew on the stem. Harvey was right. The rush was like an orgasm on acid.

"Wow," I gasped when I could speak, "it felt like the top of my head would explode." I was frightened by the intensity of the drug and mentally filed it away as just another drug experience I didn't need to repeat.

Ten years later, free-basing had been reborn as crack cocaine and when I encountered it again I was caught off guard. I had just left an AA meeting, and stopped at a Seven-Eleven, before heading home to do some wiring on our unfinished house, when I heard a familiar voice.

"Hey, Doug, long-time-no-see, man, what's up?" Harvey had left the bureau years before and I hadn't seen him since I'd met Cloudy. Harvey had always been stocky, but now he was almost skeletal. As he extended his hand I noticed several raw sores on his arm.

"Hi, Harv, I'm fine. How are you doing?"

"I'm great, just great. Hey, Doug, which way you goin'? Give me a ride out to eighty – second, okay?" It was on my way, and it seemed easier to comply. In the car Harvey pulled out a lighter and fumbled in his pocket.

"No cigarettes in the car," I cautioned.

"Sure man, this is just a little rock." He pulled out a short, blackened glass tube the diameter of a pencil. "Hey, man, stop at that park over there." He placed a dirty-white piece of what looked like quartz into one end of the glass tube and handed it to me. I stuck the other end in my mouth and took my first hit of crack in ten years. After that things progressed quickly and in a month I was getting high every weekend. The more I got, the more I craved. George Carlin put it well when he quipped, "Give me a hit of cocaine and I'm a new man. The problem is, the first thing the new man wants is another hit of cocaine."

Soon I was getting high almost every day, hemorrhaging money, and having outbursts of anger that terrified Cloudy and our daughter Tiffany, who was now two. Cloudy could see something was wrong, but I had practiced my lying for years back in Montana, so when I placed the blame on 'problems at work' she tried hard to believe me.

In fact, I was screwing up at work - typical behavior for a crackhead, and the only real surprise was that I still had a job. It helped that the performance bar at the Water Bureau was set so low that even a crackhead, if he was motivated (and believe me, I really wanted to keep those paychecks coming in) could meet their standards.

It was Cloudy, red-eyed and tight lipped, who finally confronted me one Saturday.

"Doug, I can't stand this anymore. I know you're using something," she held up her hand. "Don't bother to lie anymore, it's quite obvious. You need to go into rehab. If you care about me or your daughter you'll go, but it has to be now. I called Oak Hills Recovery and they have a vacant bed. Either go or get out." I went, and in February of 1986, about six months after Harvey gave me that hit in a Portland park, I entered rehab for the first time. I was forty years old.

Rehab was a nice vacation. The staff was sympathetic and caring, and except for Paul, my assigned counselor, easy to manipulate. After my sincere, tearful and oh-so-brave performance during my last group therapy session, Paul pulled me aside.

"You know, Doug, this isn't a game. Fooling us isn't going to help you get better."

"I know that, Paul, and I really appreciate how you call me on my games. It's hard, when you've lied as long as I have, to finally come clean and take responsibility."

"If that's what you're doing, fine. Just tell me, how are you going to stay clean when you get out?"

"You've seen my aftercare plan, right? Ninety meetings in ninety days, get a sponsor, work the steps…" Paul cut me off.

"I didn't ask you to recite the Big Book. I want to know, when you're out and you really want to get loaded and somebody offers you some crack, what will you do?"

"Gee, Paul, I don't know. How about if I don't go to crack houses? Or you could give me your home phone number, and if somebody walks up to me on the street and tries to twist my arm

I'll call you. Oh wait, once the money stops you're not interested anymore, are you?"

"You know, Doug; you're a real smart guy. You're right, I really don't give a shit about you. I just hate to see you destroy your family." Except for Paul, I think the staff was fooled.

I left rehab in March and returned to work. I went to meetings, got a sponsor, and worked the first five of AA's twelve steps. Then my recovery stalled. How could I ask God, a vague personage I no longer believed in, to remove the part of me that liked to get high?

My first relapse came that April, but it was a small one and I fell into a pattern that lasted for the next year and a half. Now and then, something would happen at home or at work to trigger my craving and I would score some crack, binge smoke it over a weekend and, full of remorse, struggle to quit again. Then, two or three or five weeks later, it would all happen again.

I told Cloudy I was staying clean, that the problem was just my job, and that things would get better. I don't think she believed me, but without evidence to the contrary she was stuck.

Chapter 22

Hot Coffee at the Lazy W

1987 – 1992 Portland

The situation at work was a legitimate mess and though I was at the eye of the problem it was not entirely due to my addiction. Because of my college degree, Fred, our new Division Manager, had me writing internal policies and procedures. For years, many areas had operated as isolated, autonomous fiefdoms and their foremen were very territorial. The new policies drew a lot of flak from field crews, foremen and supervisors, and when Fred refused to back me, I became the goat. I was furious and pretended not to care, but the pressure was building.

The situation at work exploded one rainy December afternoon in 1987 when Big Jim, one of the supervisors, stormed into my cubical. Jim, who had the build of a football lineman, had served in Vietnam, stood about 6' 4" and was known to have anger issues of his own.

"Damn it, Dodd, what are you doing messing with my crews? Chris says you shut down one of his trucks today. That was a priority job they were on. You should have asked me first."

Big Jim was not quite shouting as he loomed over me. Coffee sloshed in the cup he was carrying and I took an involuntary step backwards.

"I didn't shut down the truck, Jim. The laborer was on vacation and your mechanic didn't call in sick until after eight. By then everybody was already assigned and I didn't have any more people. Chris had two other crews and I suggested he put one of them on that job."

"I don't care, Dodd, that's my decision. You should have called me anyway."

"Jim, that was six hours ago. It's not my fault if your men don't communicate with you. I didn't sign on as a babysitter." An instant later I was wearing Jim's coffee.

I wiped my face and headed toward Fred's office. Big Jim apologized and gave me twenty dollars for the shirt, but the public humiliation burned hotter than the brew. I dug out Harvey's number, swung by his apartment after work, and traded Big Jim's twenty for a nice rock. After the first ear- ringing hit I didn't give a rat's ass about Jim or his coffee.

The next day my deliberate provocation of Jim and the seriousness of his assault hit me. Jim was dangerous; what if he had thrown more than coffee? After rehab and hundreds of twelve-step meetings, things should have been better. But the truth was I didn't want to work the program. I wanted fun. I wanted my old life back, before my marriage and my daughter. But what kind of worthless, selfish scum had those feelings? I resolved, one more time, to try something, anything, that might help.

Throughout 1988 and 1989 as I stumbled from one failed treatment to another, my relapses continued. I tried Prozac, talk therapy, Rapid Eye Movement therapy, and two sessions with an obese, weepy female family therapist who seemed even crazier than me. Any of the treatments could have helped but

I was caught in Walt Kelly's conundrum: I had met the enemy and he was me.

Cloudy and I had wanted a second child, but her first pregnancy had been so difficult we turned to adoption. The process was long and tedious, but finally in 1989, the day after Thanksgiving we went home with Nathan, our three day old son. I took four weeks off from work to care for Nate while Cloudy stayed at her job.

To say I was not a good father, is an understatement, but I tried. My mood swings, drug use and cravings eroded my patience. Fortunately our house was twenty-five miles outside Portland and I didn't know any dealers who delivered. Nate managed to survive my haphazard parenting, but I was smoking regularly. I didn't dare smoke around Cloudy so I smoked at work in my City car and to hell with the consequences. By the summer of 1990 I was spending a fourth of my salary, about nine hundred a month, on crack. Of course it wasn't enough, and of course it couldn't go on forever. If I wanted to prolong my addiction I needed more cash.

Although I was a proficient liar, I had never learned to steal. Due to this unfortunate handicap, obtaining other people's money seemed at first beyond my ability. I knew nothing about burglary, and forgery and bank robbery involved the feds – a bad thing in my opinion. Shoplifting seemed doable, but the dealers I knew wanted actual cash, not steaks, cases of beer, or clothes that didn't fit. Even if I managed to boost, say, a color television, dealers still traded at only about ten cents on the dollar. I needed to walk into a store broke and walk out with cash.

Fred Meyer, a popular chain of stores in Portland, carried a wide variety of products from groceries and garden supplies to hardware and clothing. The stores were large with multiple entrances and, best of all, every store's return desk was located near the middle of the store. Anyone with the proper receipt could walk up to the customer service counter with an item and walk out with cash.

I trolled about the stores until I found a suitable receipt, then I located the item and boldly carried it to the return desk. I only chose cash sales under fifty dollars so I didn't need to show my ID. I usually wore a suit and tie and rotated my 'shopping' from store to store. I was nervous at first but the rush of the theft became like a hit of crack. It gave me a sense of power.

Throughout 1990 and '91 I spent a lot of most workdays looking for money, buying drugs or getting high. I also had to take time out for the weekly meetings the City expected me to attend, and for less frequent interruptions – like the time I had to go downtown to pick up an award from the Bureau Administrator. I was disgusted by the cheap certificate and by the fact that these clueless upper echelon idiots had picked a crack-head for Employee of the Month. I would have preferred a twenty-dollar bill.

Chapter 23

Down in Flames

1992 – 1994 Portland

Once the ethical ice broke, I began stealing from the City as well. I took gloves, tools and any portable item that I could sell to a second-hand store. By the start of 1992 I was preying on co-workers. I rifled lockers in the employee shower room, took cash from wallets, and pilfered petty cash. Some of my thievery went unnoticed or, at least unreported, but eventually word of the thefts spread through the division and a quiet search began for the culprit.

As my scruples vanished, they were replaced by guilt and self-loathing. I couldn't justify what I was doing; I was just too selfish to stop. I expected to be caught and began to take greater and greater risks, even smoking crack in the building while I was at work.

By April, 1992, although I knew I was a junkie, I didn't know the City was about to install surveillance cameras. I was spared that exposure, and subsequent arrest, when Cloudy found my pipe and paraphernalia.

"God damn you, Doug, you worthless lying ass-hole. I got a call yesterday from Fred. He said there's been a bunch of thefts at the Bureau and you're under investigation. Now I find this!" She threw the pipe down and ground it under her work boots. "I want you out of here now!" She was screaming, tears rolling down her cheeks. "Why are you doing this to us? You're killing the kids and me and you don't even care. Go check yourself in to Providence now or I'm calling the Sheriff."

While I cowered in rehab, my future lay in the hands of attorneys. I spoke with my lawyer exactly once, just long enough to sign papers empowering her to negotiate with the City Attorney. The Bureau didn't want a scandal, I didn't want to go to jail, and since the mountain of evidence against me was almost entirely circumstantial, I was allowed to pay $5,000 in restitution and quietly resign without ever being charged with a crime. I'd been with the Bureau nineteen years.

My last week in treatment, Cloudy visited me with tears running down her cheeks and divorce papers in her hand.

"Doug, I have to do this to protect the kids. My attorney says you have to read these before you sign."

"I'm really sorry, Cloud. I don't want a divorce. Things will be better this time, you'll see. I promise. Please, I love you. Can't you just hold off for a couple months?" We were both crying now.

"It's too late. I can't believe you anymore. You've done this too many times and I just can't take the chance. Please, if you love me like you claim, you'll sign the papers."

I signed the papers unread. When Cloudy and the kids left my life, I felt like everything good went with them. All our mutual friends shunned me. When Walter learned of the divorce and my addiction, he naturally took Cloudy's side. It was fortunate for her and the kids that he did. I had drained our checking account and dipped deep into savings. Without money from Walter they would have been buried in debt. When I left rehab Cloudy retained everything except my clothes and a ten year old Toyota Tercel.

I went directly from treatment to a job with a property management company as the live-in manager of an apartment complex in central Portland. The position came with a small apartment and a miniscule salary. My annual income would be about twelve thousand dollars, a bit less than my child support obligation.

At the apartment complex I collected rent checks and performed minor maintenance. The building was old and something was always broken – a clogged toilet, a loose banister or a burned-out hall light. In the basement, every renter had a storage unit, a six by eight chicken wire enclosure so flimsy that most tenants didn't bother to affix a padlock to the hasp that secured the door.

I rifled the storage units for anything of value. In one space I unearthed a box of papers that included an old checkbook containing a half dozen unused checks. I suspected the account was defunct, so over a three day weekend when the banks were closed I turned those checks into cash at a particularly trusting store.

When I wasn't collecting rents, unclogging toilets or signing other people's bad checks, (forgery has such a negative sound), I managed to lie my way through a couple of twelve-step meetings every week and get high in between. Too fearful to pursue a truly lucrative life of crime and too messed up to get a real job, I bumbled my way pathetically through my new life. Like a moral leper, some of my misery rubbed off on everyone I touched. I was no use to anyone, with no prospects for improvement. Then, one February morning in 1994, I got a break.

"Hello. Terrace apartments. How can I help you?" Nearly all my calls were from prospective tenants, so I tried to answer the phone as I'd been instructed.

"Hey, Dodd, there's a job opening with the City of Yakima. You interested?"

"Mike?" It had been over a year since I'd heard from Mike Parsons, my old co-worker and climbing partner. Mike was the only person at the Bureau who had showed even a vestige of sympathy when I was fired.

"What kind of job are we talking about?"

"It's for a Water Superintendent and there's a description in today's Oregonian. It sounds like something you could handle."

"I would love to get back into water and I sure can't do that here. Thanks, I'll check it out."

"Look, Dodd, you really need to get squared away, stay off the dope. Anyway, I gotta go. Good luck with this. Bye."

"Goodbye, Mike. Thanks."

The job description, at least in theory, might have been written especially for me. Professional requirements – I had all the certificates, training and experience. Salary offered – slightly more than what I'd made at the Water Bureau. Duties – supervise and manage a forty-five person staff. I'd been there and done that. No mention of a required drug test – that was good too. The reference check would surely be a deal breaker. I submitted my application anyway.

Three weeks later I was in Yakima for an interview. The whole production felt like an acid trip with the Marx Brothers, perhaps because I'd smoked a little rock on the drive up from Portland. I walked in to a conference room packed with people where I needed a score-card to tell the players. I'd expected the panel to include the Chief Engineer and my prospective boss, but the heavy hitters like the Mayor and City Manager were a surprise.

Even more puzzling, were the two foremen and a secretary. They would be working directly for me, if I got the job.

After the required pleasantries they began firing questions from every side. I don't remember their questions or my answers, but by the end of the interview almost everyone was laughing. Everything had gone just a little too well. I left suspecting that something was rotten in the City of Yakima. Were they as desperate to fill the position as I?

Chapter 24

I'll Burn that Bridge when I Get to It

May, 1994, Yakima

That May, against all reason, I was offered the position. I knew there was a catch but all my other options looked worse. At lunch, my first day on the job, Ed opened the curtain on the real situation in Yakima. Ed, a big bluff fellow of about sixty, was the assistant city manager.

"There are a couple things you need to know about the situation here, Doug. Whatever you do don't ever say anything to Clarence. He hates every city employee. If you were drowning Clarence would throw you a brick." Clarence had the longest tenure of any council member and always looked like he had just bit into a lemon. He was retired and, according to Ed, had no interests outside of city business.

"Also," Ed continued, if you have any questions don't bother Dick. Talk to me." Dick, known behind his back as King Richard, had been city manager for seventeen years and knew not only where all the bodies were buried but also who had been holding the shovel. I remembered him from my job interview as one of the two people who had not been amused by my performance. Clarence had been the other.

"Now, let's get down to specifics. First off, there's Acquavella." Ed loosened his silk tie and smiled at me over the menu as the waiter arrived.

"Order what you want," Ed said, "it's on the city's dime."

After we ordered, Ed resumed his monologue. "Acquavella is a lawsuit about water rights. You'll learn all about it when you meet with the attorneys. They'll get you up to speed before you testify. Then there're the old wooden mains; you'll need some public meetings for them. Finally, you should meet with the consultant about the contaminated aquifer." Ed smiled benignly and sipped his drink.

A lawsuit, wooden mains and a contaminated aquifer? I didn't know where to begin.

Lunch ended without further bombshells, but the next day, as I read through the mountain of paper on my desk, I realized Ed had minimized the problems. The trial shaped up to be a battle royal between a half-dozen private water companies, the city, Washington State, the Army Corps of Engineers, and the Yakama Nation. Losing would be a disaster for the city.

The ancient wood mains that carried irrigation water to the residents were even older than Clarence and resembled sieves. They were so bad that only about a cup and a half of every gallon that entered the main actually reached the customer.

The area's primary aquifer had tested positive for PCB, a volatile organic chemical known to cause cancer. The water in at least eight-hundred local wells was now undrinkable.

Just in case these practical problems weren't enough, I would be facing an entrenched city council member who already thought my budget was too large. Perhaps Clarence would be kind enough to organize the public meetings Ed had mentioned. He could stand at the door and distribute torches and pitchforks.

Looking back, I can see a lot of flaws in my thinking. My job paid well, and the city provided a phone and car. My support staff was outstanding and all forty-two employees seemed competent. The three big issues Ed had mentioned, the lawsuit, the wood mains and the contaminated aquifer, were all long-term pre-existing problems.

The lawsuit seemed endless and was beyond my control anyway, so why worry? The contaminated aquifer was more of a nuisance than a threat. The city got its water from the Naches River, not wells, and with the private wells being phased out, the city was actually gaining customers, probably a good thing. The leaking wooden mains would have been replaced decades ago except for Clarence. On his watch, irrigation users had been paying ridiculously low rates, while their antiquated system deteriorated beyond repair, something my predecessor had thoroughly documented. This was Clarence's monkey, and I could make him own it.

These issues had dragged on for years, and that didn't seem likely to change. If the City chose to let me go after two or three years, so what? Yakima was a nice town and $50,000 a good annual salary. I had a second chance, something I neither expected nor deserved.

For my first month on the job I was a model employee. I learned the name and job title of each of my employees and schmoozed council members. I studied maps, pondered legal documents and inspected equipment. I toured the treatment plant and ingratiated myself with the secretaries and technicians. I gave special attention to the irrigation system and planned public meetings. I visited crews in the field. I even gave interviews to the local media. My days were a whirlwind of activity. Evenings, I read histories of the area and the town, and studied my department's budget line by line. I also stayed clean.

Alone on weekends, I worried about the job and my family. I still didn't understand the budget. What if I never got it right? Would Cloudy ever stop hating me? What was she telling Tiffany and Nate? Some nights, consumed by these thoughts, I couldn't sleep

I didn't share my fears about my family and job with anyone. I should have gone to a meeting. I didn't call Walter or my sister. I could have called Mike Parsons, my old friend who had had informed me about the vacancy to begin with. With typical addict thinking, I did none of those things. Instead, lost in self-pity, I told myself that the job was hopeless, that my kids hated me, and that I was doomed to fail.

Because I didn't look for help, I eventually looked for crack. I was ignorant of the Yakima crack scene, so help would have been easier to find, but like a good addict, I persevered.

Chapter 25

Deja Vu All Over Again

July, 1994 to August, 1995 Yakima

Around midnight, the Friday I cashed my second paycheck from the city, I sat alone at the bar in a seedy Yakima cantina staring into a mirror at a balding, middle aged white male. If I were a dealer, I'd figure this guy for a narc. I sighed and turned to the Anglo chick with long, dirty brown hair who was wiping down the bar.

"Um, can I get another beer?"

As she delivered the beer, she spoke. "So what brings you to a dump like this?"

"I've spent," I checked the time on my phone, "four hours trying to find some rock and everybody looks at me like I'm a cop." I shook my head in disgust.

"I know all the cops in this shithole of a town, so I know you're not one. These fucking Mexicans are all so paranoid. My name's Carrie, by the way."

"I'm Doug," I responded. "I moved here from Portland. Got a lot of contacts there, mostly black, and those dudes sell right on the street. Here? Shit, I don't even know where to start looking."

"Do you still want to get something?" Carrie looked at me, waiting.

"Hell yes! You know somebody?"

"Come by here," she jotted something on a napkin and handed it to me, "around noon tomorrow and I'll hook you up. Okay?"

"For sure, Carrie. Thanks."

The next day I drove four blocks from my studio apartment to the address Carrie had given me, a one bedroom roach-infested hovel where she lived with Miguel and their three preschoolers. I'd been looking all over town but had failed to check my own back yard. Miguel, about five feet tall and very dark with features hinting at a strong Indian heritage, greeted me with a complicated three-move handshake.

"Pleased to meet you, Miguel. Carrie says you might be able to get me some rock."

"Roca? No, Douglas, you go jail long time, roca. I got powder. How much you want?"

"How about forty? That's all I got right now." I'd been burned enough times back in Portland to become wary and I wanted to sample his product before risking too much cash.

In Portland I'd always bought cocaine in rock form. I knew powdered coke had to be cooked before it could be smoked, but I'd never done it myself. Miguel didn't use his own product but Carrie did and she was happy to teach me how to rock up a batch.

"It's simple. You can use either baking soda or ammonia. Ammonia's easier but be sure to rinse it good when you're done." Carrie dumped the powder I'd purchased from Miguel into a blackened metal spoon, and carefully tipped in about a quarter cap of ordinary household ammonia and held the spoon over a lighter.

"You want to keep the heat low. Now watch." As Carrie gently brought the mixture to a boil, an oily, slightly yellowish circle formed on the surface. After a few more seconds, she snapped off the lighter, picked up a nickel and dipped it directly into the oily sheen. As it cooled, the cocaine adhered to the coin, forming a hard, lumpy white mass the size of a grape.

"There you go, rinse it off in some water and you're all set," Carrie concluded as she handed me the coin. The whole process couldn't have taken over two minutes.

"Wow, Carrie that came out great." If the dope was any good, I'd just got a hell of a deal for forty bucks. I scraped the rock off the nickel onto one of my freshly printed City of Yakima business cards. I'd been straight for almost two months and I couldn't take my eyes off the pile of fresh crack. I wanted to get high and suddenly realized I didn't have a pipe. "Uh, Carrie, do you want a hit?" 'Can I borrow your pipe?' was my unspoken but understood request.

"Sure, Doug, thanks. I've got a extra stem here. You want it?"

Miguel didn't like strangers to smoke at their house, so I broke Carrie off a portion of what she had cooked up, folded the rest into a piece of paper, and hurried back to my apartment.

The first hit made my ears ring and knocked me back in my chair. Miguel's dope was as good as any I could remember at about half the Portland price. Within a couple months I was his regular customer.

After I first started using crack in Portland I had managed to hang on to my job with the city for seven years. In Yakima I lasted less than one. In Portland my decline and fall had been slowed because I usually didn't dare smoke at home. In Yakima I had an anonymous studio apartment two blocks from a Seven Eleven that featured a cash machine.

My 'geographical cure' had turned out to be just the next stage of my disease. With crack being cheaper and more potent than in Portland, my self-destruction was faster and more dramatic, and my 'bottom' – in AA speak – was lower.

I soon became acquainted with four women who were ready for anything as long as I had rock. Carrie ignored the irony of her own dependence on Miguel and referred to them as 'crack whores.' For me, any company was a step up from my own.

Flora was in her early twenties, blond, slim, and quite passive. She said little, and tended to pilfer small pieces of rock. When she was around I found myself waiting for her to leave.

Sheila was pushing forty and, unlike most crackheads, running to fat. She claimed to be from a family of well-off Yakima orchardists and frequently bemoaned her current reduced state. After we smoked up my crack Sheila would weep at the cruelty of an unjust fate or storm out into the street looking for more drugs.

Dorry was about thirty. An attractive red-head with a smart mouth, she loved to play cribbage while we smoked. She was an unmerciful tease and if she ever stole anything from me I never caught her. I wanted Dorry as my girlfriend, but our relationship was strictly business.

Mary was older still, nearly my age, and her years in the life had not been easy. Solid and drab with thin, graying hair, Mary reminded me of a peasant woman from a movie, set in the Balkans Slow, honest and eager to please, Mary was timid until she realized I didn't hit women. She was the only one of the four who ever brought me drugs. By June, 1994, after just two months in Yakima, the stage was set. Crack and I were together again and with the help of Flora, Sheila, Dorry and Mary, I began flushing my new life down the toilet.

By January 1995, I regularly ran short of cash. I started working my receipt scam at the local Fred Myer, but I wanted more. On a Friday in March I hit a local department store and was arrested by the Yakima Police. On Monday, King Richard, his face tight with fury, pulled me into his office.

"Your signature on this," he said, handing me a single typed page, "now". I don't recall the wording of my resignation, but I remember something like pain in his eyes. I had let Dick down and he took my arrest very personally.

After my termination I was temporarily flush with cash. Washington State returned the $3,500 I had paid into their retirement system and that, together with my last check from the city, came to over $7,000. As the money ran out, I stopped all my discretionary spending, beginning with my monthly car payment and child support. I managed to pay my July rent before I began hitting various ATMs with my credit cards for cash advances.

I knew what I was doing and understood where it would all lead. Hell, I wasn't stupid – I was a junkie. I was just doing what junkies did.

As all the outward trappings of my life were whittled away I felt like a spectator at a funeral that just wouldn't end. From July to November of 1995, exact dates are a mystery. I think the car went first. I remember two men came to the door with papers and I gave them the keys. I emptied a small account that I'd forgotten at the credit union. When bills arrived I threw them in the trash. Somehow I found myself in a different apartment in the same complex. At some point both of my credit cards stopped working and the first eviction notice arrived.

In October, I got caught shoplifting again. I remember being grabbed by the store security guard, a young sweating kid in his twenties, who put me in some sort of wrist lock. I remember breaking away and running for about a block, looking back and seeing him puffing gamely along behind. The silly bastard just wouldn't give up, so I stopped and waited for him.

"Okay I won't run anymore," I told him.

"You run pretty fast for an old guy," he said, and we walked back to the store together.

I remember being booked at the city's fine new jail, and seeing the judge. I recall telling her I was an addict; then weeping and thanking her as I wept, for putting me in jail. My two weeks in the 'pod' consisted of hours of mind numbing boredom, interrupted occasionally by the impersonal cruelty of several young white punks. Some older Mexican gentlemen (who adamantly did not wish to be called Hispanic) shared their food with me. Upon my release I walked back to my apartment and found Mary waiting.

I didn't want to go back to jail so I quit shoplifting. A few weeks later, just before Thanksgiving, Mary left on a Greyhound for her sister's in Spokane and I headed for the Mission.

CHAPTER 26

BACKSLIDING INTO RECOVERY

1997 TO 2000 YAKIMA

Since I first stumbled into the mission in November of 1995, a lot had changed. The longer I worked for the Wolffs, the less patience I had with mission life. Line guys repeatedly asked me for money or tried to sell me drugs and the trainees treated me with contempt. Near the end of December 1997 I went to see Ellery in his office.

"How are you doing, Doug? You've been on the Line for almost a year and a half. Have you thought it over and decided to rejoin the Program?"

"We've been over this before, Ellery, I can't afford the Program. I'm not keeping up with my child support as it is, but at least I can pay something. I came here because Scotty has started giving me a new bed assignment every night. That way I don't get clean sheets. I don't think that's fair."

"I don't know anything about that." Ellery shook his head.

"Okay, Rod has me empty the garbage and wash out all the cans every afternoon for my bed-work. It takes me two hours even if I hurry. Do you know of any other Line guy who has to work that much for their bed?"

Scotty and Rod were both second year trainees. When I'd been acting kitchen manager I'd had conflicts with both when I caught them taking food I'd set aside for special meals. Now they were making me pay. Ellery had always seemed like a fair person. How would he react?

"That's news to me," he responded. "I do know that Line guys never seem to get better."

"Maybe Line guys don't get better because staff doesn't want them to. If I do okay on the Line it makes your program look bad. Now I tell you Scotty and Rod are harassing me and you don't know anything. Maybe you don't want to know."

Ellery folded his arms across his chest and looked down.

"You need to find another place to live. You've got two weeks." He didn't meet my eyes.

I didn't know what else to do, so that weekend I called Dad in Montana. As we talked, memories of life on the ranch came flooding back and it struck me that my dad, the quiet, devout Scottish teetotaler had a lot in common with Dick Wolff the loud, profane, beer-swilling German. They were both ridiculously strong and hardworking, and neither ever asked me to do anything he wouldn't do himself. They were also surprisingly compassionate. After I explained the situation to Dad, he agreed to help with my rent. Two days ahead of Ellery's deadline, I moved into a one room shack three blocks from the Mission.

In my shack, away from the mission, it was easy to smoke but crack was becoming a disappointment. While I was still rushing from my first hit, my mind would fill with a vague, free-floating anxiety that something really bad was about to happen. I huddled in my shack, unable to endure being around people, yet fearfully alone with my thoughts. Work became the best part of my life, and though I still smoked occasionally, my high was never very satisfying.

Thanks to Wolff's Wood Work and my father, I made it through the winter. In the spring work picked up, and by May of 1998 I was working full time. Then, in July, Greg Wolff got married and bought out his father. I immediately liked Julie, Greg's new wife. She was cheerful, intelligent, and with a degree in accounting, had very firm ideas about how to run a company. Big changes were in store for the Wolffs, and I wondered about my place in the new order.

Greg called his new company Wolff's Tree Service, gave me a pay raise and began following all the rules. He bought all new safety gear and upgraded some old vehicles. Because I could no longer drive, I worked fewer hours.

I hardly saw Dick the summer of '98. I spent a lot of time with Greg on twenty-acres of hillside property a couple miles east of Yakima. That fall contractors threw up a high-ceilinged one-hundred-foot square shop, and in March of '99 started work on what promised to be a three or four-million-dollar house. Greg and Julie let me stay in Greg's small motor home on the property. There I could watch the construction site overnight and walk to work in the morning.

My bond with Greg and Julie was strong but reality kept intruding. I couldn't get a driver's license till I paid $2,000 in fines. My back child support was now around $50,000. The months went by and their new house neared completion. Soon my night watchman's duties would end. The tree service could still use me part time, but my usefulness was limited. The Wolffs had carried me long enough.

Over the 2000 fourth of July weekend, out of boredom or loneliness or compulsion, I had my last relapse. It was a total disaster. The first puff filled me with a surge of paranoia. I was sure something awful - I didn't know what - was about to happen. The cops were about to break in. My heart was about to explode. My high was ruined. I felt caught between my paranoia and my addiction.

Once my rock was gone, I was wracked with guilt. I needed to stay clean and start paying back child support. Crack was ubiquitous in Yakima, and I didn't trust my resolve, so I decided to look for jobs out of town.

In November, Trident Seafoods held interviews at the Yakima Red Lion for seafood processors in Alaska. I filled out an application, took a physical exam and gave a urine sample. Later I told Greg what I was contemplating.

"Alaska, huh? Travis was always flapping his gums about working as a deckhand on a crab boat. What are you gonna do there?"

"I don't have the job yet. The company has shore plants and processor ships. They fish for Pollock, whatever that is. They have all kinds of work. The season lasts about three months, then there's a break. They pay $6.75 an hour plus board and room, and there's supposed to be overtime."

"What if you get there and don't like it? Or you're seasick all the time. You can't walk back."

"Greg, I have to get out of Yakima. If Trident hires me, I'll stick it out, do whatever it takes. You guys have been great, but it's time for me to leave."

In December, I got a letter from Trident offering a job in their Akutan plant and instructing me to report to their Seattle office the first week in January. I said good-bye to the Wolffs and then stopped by to see Kermit and Carol. They asked me to stay for dinner and Kermit took me into his office to talk.

"I always wanted to see Alaska, but I doubt it'll happen now, at my age. Do you know where you'll be working?"

"A place called Akutan. I looked at a map and didn't see it so I don't know."

"Let's see." Kermit pulled out a folded wall map and laid it out on the floor. "Looks like it's an island out on the Aleutian Chain right…here," he pointed with his finger. "It's pretty small so probably no roads, but this shows a village so there may be some people there."

"I'll be there for three or four months. They didn't say exactly how long."

"Wonder what they mean by processing?" Kermit mused.

"I don't know. It doesn't really matter," I shrugged, "a job is a job."

I called Cloudy with the news and exchanged awkward good-byes with Tiffany and Nathan. They had turned seventeen and eleven in November and I hadn't sent presents. Now I would be thousands of miles away for months. I doubted they would notice.

I was very apprehensive all that last week. I wanted a hit. In my dreams, I put chunks of rock in a pipe and flicked the lighter. I heard the sizzle, saw the smoke, inhaled…and woke up shaking and covered with sweat. I hated what I had become and prayed, for the first time in forever, that Alaska would be more than just another futile, geographical cure.

Chapter 27

The Fifty-Five-Year-Old Greenhorn

January 2001 Akutan, Alaska

I caught the Greyhound to Seattle on a crisp, gray January morning, everything I owned in a backpack and duffle. There was room left over. I remembered fleeing Missoula in a bus ahead of the police thirty years before. Santayana could have had me in mind when he noted that someone who can't remember the past is doomed to repeat it. Apparently I was a slow learner.

Three flights and thirty hours later, I sat next to the pilot in a pontoon-equipped Grumman Goose headed east out of Dutch Harbor. The Goose droned deafeningly through a stark, off-white world and soon reached an island with an obvious volcanic cone and a deep bay ringed by steep, snow-capped mountains. I could see a complex of two and three story structures squeezed between bay and mountain. Tanks, some that might hold a million gallons, dotted the site. A score of boats were tied up along a dock that ran the length of the complex. Just past the end of the dock, shipping containers stacked three or four high, littered the shore. Farther east, toward the mouth of the bay, a sprawl of much smaller structures formed what I guessed was the village. It was otherworldly and beautiful.

The Goose settled smoothly onto the water, taxied to shore and, shedding water, rolled up onto a macadam pad. After the plane's two engines died, I got out ahead of the other passengers, four short brown men who chattered excitedly in a language I didn't recognize, and a dark, quiet couple who didn't speak at all. A John Deere ATV rolled up a rough track from the east; an old woman stepped off and boarded the Goose. The quiet couple climbed on the ATV which wheeled about and headed back toward the village. The Goose came alive, taxied back into the bay, and with a sudden roar, rose, spiraled upwards, and disappeared. Except for the four brown men, no one else had spoken a word. A battered green Suburban arrived from the west and I piled in with the others.

As we approached the Plant, a dull, big-engine rumble filled my ears. That omnipresent drone was the life force of the Plant. For over 1,000 employees, that noise represented more than just the power that operated the machines that provided our paychecks. All our heat, light, food and water depended on that noise, as did our contact with the outside world.

At least one of the plant's four generators ran continuously and its background thrum became so normal that when a relay failed a few months later, and all the generators died at once, I didn't immediately understand what had happened until I saw the blue-clad figures sprinting toward the generator house. Though unnerving, these sudden power losses were rare and brief, so I ceased to give them much thought.

At full capacity, the Plant could process two million pounds of Pollock a day, and the ceasless, throbbing rhythm of the generators was overlaid by a soundtrack unique to each part of the complex. Dozens of pumps, motors, compressors, and conveyors each provided their own rattle, whine or hum. Every forklift, backhoe and truck had a back-up alarm that beeped, shrieked or squealed.

The five hulking projects-style bunkhouses had their own rhythm. Inside, movie soundtracks mingled with raised voices from round- the-clock gambling marathons and domestic disputes. In the galley, the clatter of dishes and the jangle of silver competed with the animated symphony of voices speaking Tagalog, Spanish and Vietnamese. English was the official tongue, but for most of the processors it was a second or even third language.

The morning after I arrived, I reported to the break room at the old plant where a husky blond in his late twenties with the look of a California surfer dude, was handing out paperwork. I tried to line up with a couple dozen other newbies and was immediately frustrated. To me a line was orderly, something straight out of Euclid. Here a line was like an amoeba as people crowded together, pushing, shoving and invading what I thought of as my 'personal space'.

"Listen up guys," the surfer dude began, "my name's Steve. You all need to fill out the questionnaire and a W-4 so you can get paid. If you have any special skills, like forklift driver write that down on the back. There's no fish for a few days. See me if you need something."

I don't recall the contents of the questionnaire, but on the back I put down all my experience with water systems. Although I hired on as a fish processor, saw and, oh-my-god yes, smelled fish every day on Akutan, I never touched a fish outside the galley. For this blessing, I thank Steve. I caught up with him outside the old plant after orientation to plead my case.

"Ah, Steve do you have a minute? You said to see you if we needed something before the fish come in? Well, I need something to do. I'm here to work and I'll do anything. I put down all my experience on that form. I work hard and learn fast."

"Let me think a sec." Steve stared into space and then pointed at a nearby metal clad building. "Okay, see that warehouse? Get a broom from the storeroom and sweep the second floor. Tell the storeroom I said to give you a broom. Let me know when you get done." I nodded assent and turned to walk off.

"Hey, wait," Steve called, "what's your name again?"

"Doug. Doug Dodd." Steve nodded and we went our separate ways.

The warehouse was a sty so I decided to do both floors. Even so, by mid-afternoon I was done, and judging by how dirty I was, the warehouse had to be much improved. I located Steve outside the main office.

"Steve, I swept both floors. Do you have anything else for me?" Steve gave me a puzzled look

"Dave, right?"

"It's Doug." I was patient but determined. I wanted Steve to remember me.

"Okay, Doug. On the questionnaire you filled out you said you worked with water, right?" I nodded. "Well I was talking to Charlie, he's the chief engineer, and he needs a man at the wastewater treatment plant. His office is on the second floor of the new plant. Be there at 4:30 this afternoon and I'll introduce you." Before I could voice my thanks, Steve was gone. His surfer persona was deceptive; apparently, below the surface, lurked a young man on the way up.

At 4:25 I was waiting, freshly showered, outside the office of Charles McDonald, Trident's chief engineer. There was no sign of Steve, but inside, hunched behind a desk, a man with sparse grey hair and bifocals labored over a voluminous set of blueprints. He flipped from page to page in the plans and finally, with an explosive 'Bullshit!" flung the whole set to the floor and stood glowering, massaging his lower back. This seemed like a bad time for a job interview but as I edged away from his door, he glared at me and beckoned.

"You the water guy Steve told me about?" He towered over me and enveloped my hand in a calloused paw that didn't fit my image of an engineer.

"Yes sir. I've worked with water systems for over twenty years."

"Humph. What kind of water?"

"Potable water. I started as a laborer, then an operating engineer and worked my way up to supervisor."

"Know anything about motors, pumps and valves? How about wastewater?"

"I've worked with all that stuff, but not for waste water. I learn fast, and with a few days of training I'm sure I can handle it."

"The wastewater treatment plant is a one-man show, but its 24-7 and I need a guy to pull the 6 pm to 6am shift. We have a package system, treats the domestic sewage for over a thousand people. You ever use a microscope?"

"In high school biology."

"You'll need to look at water samples under a microscope, identify organisms, that sort of thing. Oh, yeah, how are you with tests? We need a certified operator and Rudy – well he's a good man, but he's Filipino and all the tests are in English – and he just can't pass the test."

"I'm good with tests if I know what to study. That should be no problem."

"Okay, Doug, job's yours if you want it. Show up here tomorrow morning at six. I'll introduce you to Rudy."

As I walked out at 4:35, I met Steve in the hallway.

"Sorry I'm a little late. You ready to go talk to Charlie?"

"I already talked to Charlie and I start tomorrow. That was the shortest job interview I've ever had. Thanks a lot Steve."

"Sure thing. See you around."

That night my elation was tempered by worry. I had assured Charlie that I could 'handle it' but was that true? For three months I would be trapped on this island, an outsider in a culture I didn't understand and, so far, didn't like. At fifty-five, I had no bridges left to burn. This was my last chance and I couldn't afford to fail.

Wastewater treatment took place in an unheated sixty by one-hundred foot metal building on the eastern edge of the Trident complex. The building held four open tanks. The tanks were huge, twelve feet high at least, and like some of the Trident supervisors, full of shit. It was my job to monitor, stir, test, treat and ultimately discharge the resulting water into the bay. Much of my work was housekeeping. Every night I hosed off floors, catwalks and walls. I ran tests, recorded results and added buckets and bags of chemicals accordingly.

With almost no training, I certainly wasn't an adequate operator so I depended on Rudy Casino, my daytime counterpart, for direction. Rudy, despite a lack of education and a poor command of English, was a great operator. If a tank smelled wrong or looked unhealthy, Rudy knew what to do without the benefit of books or even the microscope we were supposed to rely on. I was smart enough to rely on Rudy and he never steered me wrong.

Working for the engineers was a huge step up from processing, even though the hourly pay was the same. Instead of being crammed together with three or four men, I shared a room with one welder who worked the day shift, so I mostly had the place to myself. I worked twelve hours a day seven days a week which came out to eighty-four hours a week. Figuring time and a half for overtime, I grossed around $3,000 a month. Trident provided boots and raingear, and I'd arrived on Akutan with a toothbrush, toothpaste, shampoo and soap, so my expenses that first month weren't just low, they were non-existent. I no longer had a bank account, so I sent my first check to Julie Wolff back in Yakima who had agreed to hold it and front me spending money.

The Trident company store did a thriving business in phone cards, videos, cigarettes and junk food among the processors. The Galley served four full meals a day, I had no one to call and since I was a non-smoker without a video player, the store had little to offer. In the galley and the bunkhouse I still stood out but I began to see the stares I drew as curious rather than hostile. The greenhorn was adapting.

CHAPTER 28

THE PLANT, THE VILLAGE, THE ISLAND

FEBRUARY, 2001 AKUTAN

"You could hear a lot better without those damn things!" It was midnight in the galley and I flushed and yanked off my ear protectors. The speaker, a stubby engineer I'd seen but had not met, set his tray on the table across from me and plopped onto the bench. The treatment plant was unheated as well as noisy, so the heavy muffs served a dual purpose, but I still felt a fool.

"God, I'm sick of pineapple," he continued, mumbling past a piece of bacon and scowling at me. "I think these damn Filipino cooks would put it in the oatmeal if they thought of it. Fish, coleslaw, salad, cake – everything."

"A meal every six hours is confusing" I responded. "Between the rice and pineapple and my shift I don't know whether I'm eating breakfast or dinner, but I mostly like the food."

"Just wait, you haven't been here long enough." He stuck out a greasy hand. "Mike Johnson. Where you from?"

"Doug Dodd, and I was raised up in Montana."

"Hey men, mind if I join you?" I'd met Carl Erickson, the assistant chief engineer, but other than noticing he walked with a limp, I'd formed no real impression.

"Sure, grab a seat," I responded. "It's good to speak English with somebody. So, what do you guys do here besides work, eat and sleep?"

"Not much," Mike replied. "You can go to the village but they don't like us. There's the Roadhouse if you like to drink but it's really depressing." Mike stood up and stretched. "I can't eat this junk, see you guys later."

"So is this place as bad as Mike says?" I asked Carl.

Carl sat, carefully adding sugar to his oatmeal, and not answering. On closer examination he looked to be about my age though taller, with a graying beard. I saw he wore a hearing aid and wondered if he'd heard me. Finally, he looked up.

"Mike's wrong about the villagers. They aren't unfriendly, just careful. They're Aleuts and they've been burned a lot; first by the Russians, then by the army in WWII and now by the processors. They're pretty quiet, but they have some interesting material in their library. If you're patient, they'll show it to you."

"I love to read. Where's the library?"

"Go past the Trident Church – that's the big white building near where the Goose lands. Take the middle boardwalk. Go past the Roadhouse, the Akutan store, and the post office. Pass the Russian Orthadox church and on the left you'll see a big gray building. That's city hall. The library is past city hall on your left. If you get to the generator shed you've gone too far."

"What about the island? What's it like?" I asked this in all innocence, but Carl stared at me in silence for so long I wondered if I had offended him in some way. Then he recited as though reading from a guidebook.

"The treeless island of Akutan is in the Aleutian chain a mere 150 miles west of the Alaskan peninsula and though it is only about fifteen miles long and six wide, it covers almost 130 square miles. Volcanic action and the harsh storms have created thousands of gullies, valleys, meandering streams, gulches, waterfalls, knife edge ridges and other impediments to ground travel. Away from the native Aleut village and the fish processing plant there are no established roads and few trails. The hills rise quickly from the shore to over a thousand feet, and culminate at the 4,275 foot summit of Mount Akutan, an active volcano. The island is a naturalist's paradise with dozens of plants in the tundra alone and ten varieties of edible berries. It is also home to fox, ptarmigan, hundreds of bald eagles and a herd of feral cows". Carl dropped his professorial tone and pointed at his right foot where I noticed a heavy, re-enforced boot, "This island is an amazing place," Carl said, his tone somewhere between longing and bitter. "If I didn't have this, I'd be all over it."

I felt like a fool. Handicapped by his foot, Carl could only experience the island second hand and he obviously regretted it, something I should have figured out. Still, my curiosity overcame my embarrassment.

"I love to hike," I stated. "Are you serious about the feral cattle?"

"Well of course I've never seen 'em, but that's the story. Supposedly they hang out on the other side of the island in Hot Springs Bay. You should check it out; take pictures."

"Thanks, Carl, I will. I need to get back to work but it sounds really cool. See you around."

A few days later, around noon, I walked past the boxy Trident church into the village. Beyond the post office, on a plot of land enclosed by a white picket fence, a tiny white building stood amidst a field of wooden crosses. I peered inside the church and glimpsed exotic icons and unusual crosses. I guessed it was there that the villagers worshiped, married and took communion before making their final journey to the graveyard outside. Old but well cared for, the building and cemetery told me faith was an important part of the Aleuts' lives.

I followed the boardwalk through the village, and nodded at the people I passed. They didn't speak or make eye contact and I felt like a trespasser. The library the door was locked, and with no sign indicating hours, I headed back toward the plant. As I passed the Roadhouse, a storm hit.

It is hard to exaggerate the extremes of Aleutian weather. A day can go from clear, calm and hot to rainy, windy and cold in a matter of minutes. As I neared the Trident Church I plunged into my first williwaw – a sudden wind that seems to blow in all directions at once – and it stole my breath. Sleet stung my face and covered my glasses, effectively blinding me and I stumbled into the church to catch my breath. As I was gathering myself, a voice rang out.

"Welcome, come in and dry off." A stocky brown haired man, two inches shorter and at least twenty years younger than I, stood beneath a basketball hoop holding a ball.

"Thanks. I was looking for sanctuary but it looks like I found a gymnasium," I managed.

"I'm Pastor Dan," he laughed, "and you can take your pick. I don't get many visitors here, let alone lost sheep."

"Good to meet you, my name's Doug and I'm not exactly lost, just misplaced. How in the world did this church get here? It looks like it should be in the mid-west someplace."

"You're not far off. It's non-denominational Protestant but I think it's patterned after a Methodist church in Kansas. Trident built it at company expense and brought me here on a three-year contract. Besides this gym, it has a sanctuary that seats a hundred."

"Wow, that's pretty ambitious. Do you like it here?"

"Well," Pastor Dan looked at me and sighed, "that's a really good question. Would you like a cup of coffee?"

"Thanks, I have to be back to work at six, but I've got a little time." Dan fetched two cups and we sat in the gym on folding chairs and chatted while I dried off.

"I came here from Iowa two and a half years ago with my wife and daughter thinking there was a real need and that it would be an adventure." Dan let out a sigh and shook his head. "Both those things are true but not in the ways we expected."

"I've only been here a month but the villagers don't seem very friendly."

"Nearly all the villagers are Russian Orthodox and they have their own church. They've been either ignored or exploited for longer than any of them have been alive, so they were real skeptical when Trident built this. Some of the boys from the village come here now and then to play a little basketball, but that's about it."

"How about the processors, any interest there?"

"Not much." Dan shook his head again. "They're mostly from the Philippines, which are eighty percent Roman Catholic. A lot of them speak very little English. They come here expecting Mass and leave disappointed. The ones who aren't Catholic are a mix of Buddhists, Hindus and animists. One guy last summer asked me for a copy of the Koran! I thought he was putting me on at first. I'm not a fundamentalist, but there's got to be a line somewhere. What's next, Satanists?"

"Sounds like a really tough gig, Rev," I said, deadpan. Pastor Dan stared at me open-mouthed, and then burst into laughter.

"You're funny, Doug. I'm supposed to be listening to your troubles. Yeah, it's a tough gig, but compared to what our Lord went through it's a cakewalk. Thanks for reminding me. So tell me, what are you doing on this rock?"

"Trying to climb out of a hole I dug myself into, I guess. I'm doing water treatment for Trident and trying to find something to keep me sane. I've worked twenty-eight twelve-hour night shifts without a day off and I probably have sixty or seventy more to go. I need the money, but I have to find something to take my mind off the job and the isolation. I'd hike around the island but the steep hills and snow are a bad combination."

"You know how to use snowshoes?" Dan asked.

"Sure, we had some old 'Bear Paws' on our ranch in Montana and later I used some in Oregon. Snowshoes would be perfect. But nobody sells them here and I couldn't afford it anyway. I'll hike when the snow melts."

"You don't have to wait that long. I've got a pair of snowshoes you can borrow. They're packed away, but come back in a couple days and you can pick them up."

"Wow, thanks Dan, that would be great."

Outside the church the wind was steady from the west and as I leaned into the blow I glimpsed brown shapes moving in the bay to my left. Squinting, I saw, not far from shore, my first Stellar sea lions. About the size of horses, they looked almost mythic and I froze in awe. By the time I struggled back to the Plant my face and fingers were numb but my mind was clear. I felt energized by the cold beauty of this desolate rock and encouraged my conversation with Pastor Dan.

Within the following week, I revisited Dan. His snowshoes were aluminum with crampon type insteps and over the next weeks I slogged up the hills behind the plant and village.

The next plane brought a package from Cloudy. Instead of berating me for my many mistakes, she sent stamped envelopes and a copy of Alaska Trees and Shrubs. As I paged through the guide, and studied pictures of blueberry bushes, I wondered how much had really changed. Besides a job, I now had friends. I had been clean over six months and for the first time in years, I could start supporting Cloudy and the kids. I was still an addict, but my cravings were less intense. Surely, things were looking better, weren't they? Shit, what was I thinking? I'd watched this movie before and the hero always died at the end. I couldn't afford to hope; it was too soon to be sure. A relapse now would be too much to bear.

Chapter 29

Conversations and Cows

March, 2001 Akutan

"Well, I made it to the library but it was locked. Nobody in the village will tell me what's up." It was a slow night. Carl and I were in the galley, lingering over cherry pie and coffee.

"Let me give you a little more local history," Carl said. "The library is open. They used to leave the door unlocked and you could just walk in and check out books, videos, whatever. But many Trident workers damaged items, or didn't bring them back at all, and the villagers started keeping the door locked."

"I get that, and it makes sense; but if it's open, what's the secret?"

"There's somebody there evenings and Saturday afternoons," Carl continued, "so keep knocking till they get tired of the noise. Then you'll just have to talk your way in. The Aleuts are good people - just shy."

"Okay, thanks, I'll try that. You know some guys around the Plant have mentioned those wild cows you told me about, but they've never seen them either. Were you really serious, or is that like an island myth?"

"I have it on good authority. Some family brought them here thirty or forty years ago in hopes of starting a ranch. The villagers know. You need to get them to talk.

The next Saturday afternoon I knocked persistently on the library door. After a couple minutes a young woman opened the door.

"Can I help you?"

She didn't meet my gaze, but I was used to that.

"Hi. I really want to learn more about the island, maybe look at some maps. Is there any chance I can do that?"

"You can browse, but I can't loan you any books."

"That's alright, when are you open?"

"You can come in now, I'll be here for another hour," she replied. "The maps are over there and we just got the Xerox machine fixed so if you want copies they are a quarter each." This had turned into my first actual conversation with a villager and I was unreasonably elated. Perhaps next time there would be eye contact?

I copied a couple maps, paid, thanked her and left. At my next visit a week later we exchanged names and Tina became almost friendly.

"What kind of information are you looking for?" Tina asked.

"A guy at the plant says there are wild cows on the island and if that's true I was wondering how they got here."

"I've heard that," Tina admitted, "but I don't really know. You should ask at the post office." My conversations with Tina began a gradual thaw in my relationship with the villagers. When I said hello to people I passed on the boardwalk, some – not all – nodded in return.

A few days later I stopped by the post office and mentioned my interest in the cows to the island's postmistress. Present at the time was a hulking Native man I had previously noticed elsewhere in the village. The postmistress glanced over at him.

"I think Frank might know about the cows," she suggested. I eyed him skeptically. He looked a bit younger than I and stood well over six feet. With his full, scraggly black beard, he looked like an eighth of a ton of bad news ready to fall on me. Cautiously I extended my hand.

"Hello, my name's Doug. Do you know about the cows?"

"Frank," he confirmed softly, as he shook my hand gently. "They call me Fat Frank, and yeah, I seen the cows. They hang out over in Hot Springs Bay, mostly."

"So they're real!" I was excited. "When did they get here?"

"A long time ago, over thirty years. I was a lot younger then," he replied vaguely.

"Well who brought them here?" I was pressing, and Frank turned away.

"Charlie Brown, but he's dead. I have to go home now," he murmured.

As Frank headed for the door, I wondered what kind of cows could survive in this harsh environment. To see for myself, I'd need to hike to Hot Springs Bay.

Chapter 30

The Hills Go on Forever

April - May 2001 Akutan

By mid-April, after almost one hundred consecutive night shifts, my life had settled into a pattern: off work at six, asleep by seven, then up around noon. After lunch, things depended on the weather. If we had driving rain, or sleet, or snow I'd read and nap the afternoon away. If the storm eased, I might bundle up in my raingear and extra-tuffs and trek to the church's gym. On the rare good days, now that the snow was gone, I took short hikes up the hill behind the plant.

Saturday afternoons, storm or no, I walked to the village library, where I read and conversed with Tina and anyone else who was willing. I had yet to confirm Fat Frank's story about wild cows lurking in Hot Springs Bay and I wondered if the story was the island's equivalent of the urban alligator-in-the-toilet myth. I felt compelled to find out.

Finally, on a decent day near the end of April, I arose before noon, geared up and headed off to find the cows – if they existed. As I walked toward the head of the bay, fog still shrouded the hills. Although it wasn't raining, everything - rocks, driftwood, debris, discarded fishing gear, even the air - was wet. The slime-covered rocks along the shore were slick and I walked carefully, head down. Farther along the shore, the hills became cliffs and the Plant's perpetual generators became inaudible. Two bald eagles erupted from the fog and swooped six feet over my head. The still air magnified the sound from their huge wings and I laughed in delight.

At the head of the bay a small creek emerged from the willows. I followed it and almost immediately began to struggle. I'd hiked with Cloudy in the Pacific Northwest. We had forded streams and fought our way through slide alder, vine maple and devil's club, but nothing had prepared me for Akutan. To the eye, the gently rolling terrain looked inviting, but the tundra masked the hummocks and hid the water filled potholes. The creek followed a serpentine path and looked narrow enough to step or jump across. Often though, a cut-bank gave way under my boots and I lost my balance and plunged into water above my knees. Soaked, and facing thick fog, I grew frustrated. I was sweating, yet as soon as I stopped I grew chilled. My climbing experience told me it was time to quit and I turned back toward the plant.

That evening in the galley, I explained my problem to Carl and Mike.

"It's like trying to hike through a brush pile in a swamp! There's water everywhere, the willows hide the potholes and I'm already off balance. I really need an alpenstock."

"How about a shovel handle with, like, a spike?" Carl suggested.

"Yeah, that might work."

"Just get me the handle," Mike offered, "I'll take it from there."

A week later, as promised, Mike presented me with the finished product. I was eager to try it out. I reached the head of the bay the next day around two o'clock, and plunged into the rank Aleutian summer growth. Mike's shovel-handle alpenstock was strong enough to support my weight and the spike gave good purchase. It was just what I needed.

By then it was the first week in May, and with fifteen hours of daylight, the hills had greened up astoundingly. Berry bushes and willows, almost unnoticeable on my previous trip, had appeared out of nowhere. In a few weeks they had sprung up over a foot and their stalks dripped with condensed fog. There were also nettles and a tall, broad leafed plant I'd never seen before.

I broke out of the willows and nettles and began climbing a rocky 45-degree slope that led to an east-west ridge. I crested the ridge and paused, panting. The drop in front of me was even steeper than what I had just climbed.

Looking down, I saw what looked like a rectangular, grassy meadow, enclosed on three sides by mountains and bordered on the fourth by the sea. Without trees or some familiar object to give me a sense of scale, elevation and distance were hard to estimate. However, my map told me I stood over five hundred feet above Hot Springs Bay. Far below and to my right, I could see a sprinkling of tiny brown dots near the water. Could those be cows?

I checked the time. It was nearly 3:45. I stared down again at the dots. Cows or not, I didn't have time to satisfy my speculations. I had to be at work in just over two hours and the descent to the head of the bay, plus the shoreline hike to the Plant, would take something over an hour. If I wanted to change clothes and eat before my shift started, I had go now. There was never enough time.

As I hustled back to the Plant a thought hit me. Alone, in this strange harsh place, working long hours for low pay, I had just enjoyed a wonderful afternoon. I was not merely getting by, I was, if only briefly, happy. Something in me had changed.

A few days later Charlie McDonald called me into his office.

"You've worked over a hundred straight shifts and it's time for a break. I haven't had any complaints." He said this almost accusingly, as though he had expected less from me. "Go see Donna in the office, get your ticket, sign some papers and pick up your check. You leave May 21st and I'll need you back here around the first of June, okay?"

"Okay Boss, see you then." I had expected to be off longer, and more advance notice would have been nice, but it really didn't matter. Nobody was eagerly looking forward to my return, and I had nowhere to go. I decided to ask Cloudy if I could visit Tiffany and Nathan.

There was no cell phone service on the island, and no phones in the bunkhouse, although their arrival was rumored to be immanent. Therefore I, and one thousand processors, shared the six pay phones clustered outside the main office. There were no booths or seats, and all six were jammed into a ten by ten windowless room. The phones were notoriously unreliable, but this time my call went right through.

"Hello, Cloud, it's me. How are you guys?"

"Let's see. Tiffany is smoking pot, lying about it and being a little bitch. She's just like you and it's driving me crazy. Nathan was suspended from school again and I've got a cold. Oh yeah, I don't have any money and you owe me about a million bucks. Other than that things are great. Why are you calling?"

"Trident has been withholding $1,500 a month child support for the last three months. Didn't the state send it to you?"

"I got something from them today that I haven't had time to open yet, let me check." Pause. "Yeah, it says they made a deposit to my account. It took them long enough. You still haven't told me what this call is about."

"Trident is giving me a little time off. They'll fly me to Seattle. I'd like to catch a bus to Portland, spend some time with you and the kids if that would work for you."

"Where would you stay? You can't stay in the house."

"I know, but how about the cabin?"

"It's still there and the roof doesn't leak. You understand if I do agree to this it's for the kids' sake, right?"

"I get that. I could maybe do some stuff around your place; help with firewood or whatever you need."

"There's plenty to do and I have to work all the time just so we can eat. I didn't get any money from you for two years and you still owe me over $50,000 in back support. The little work you might do won't change that."

"Look Cloudy, I know what I've done and I can only guess how hard it's been for you. I'll pay my own expenses when I'm there. I'm clean and plan to stay that way and I thought you might let me see the kids."

"I suppose. But my place, my rules and just for one week. I don't trust you, Doug."

"I know. I should get into Portland about May 24th. I'll call you when I know for sure. Thanks for doing this."

"I just hope I don't regret it."

Cloudy's open hostility reminded me how badly I'd messed up, not just my life, but my family's as well. On Akutan I was a productive employee and, I thought, a decent person. In Portland, especially in her eyes, I was still scum. Had I really started to change or was it illusion? When I hit Portland, would I succumb to the pull of crack …again? At the treatment plant, standing atop a 50,000-gallon tank of crap, I asked God to tell me what to do and to give me the strength to do it. If there was an answer it was blocked by my ear muffs and swallowed up by the roar of the pumps and motors.

Chapter 31

Wreckage from My Past

Late May, 2001 Akutan, Portland, Akutan

On May 20, I finished my one-hundred-thirty-first consecutive graveyard shift and walked past the engineer's office toward the galley. Carl stumped down the steps and fell in beside me.

"Looks like a two-eagle day," he greeted. "We'll have a plane for sure."

"Hope so," I replied.

Weather forecasts for the Aleutians were unreliable so Carl had developed his own system that relied on the roosting habits of the bald eagles that frequented the plant. The high point of the compound was a soaring radio mast and, according to Carl, two eagles perched on that mast guaranteed that a plane could get through that day. On a one-eagle day planes were doubtful. On a no-eagle day, forget it. Although Carl wouldn't or couldn't explain his system, it seemed more accurate than official forecasts.

It was indeed a two-eagle day, and by eleven I could hear the drone of the Goose before it swooped to a landing on the nearly calm waters of the bay. Although the weather was perfect, the Goose was not, and on landing the pilot informed us that he was unable to take off because one of the side windows had developed a crack and popped out during the descent. Bear, one of the natives, grabbed the cracked Plexiglas, hopped on his ATV and roared off to the village. The other would-be passengers and I worried away a half hour till Bear returned carrying a window-shaped piece of plywood and a roll of duct tape. The pilot taped the plywood in place and pointed me to the adjacent seat.

"Just kind of push on it. It'll be fine. This ain't the first time she's lost a feather." Forty noisy, drafty minutes later we were on the ground in Dutch.

My next three flights were uneventful, and that evening I landed in Yakima where I spent the night with the Wolffs. It was good to see them, but I was uncomfortable in Yakima where I knew so many places to score drugs. In the morning Julie and I went to her bank and she persuaded them to set up a savings account in my name despite my bad credit and I deposited my Trident checks. The same afternoon I boarded a bus for Portland.

When I arrived, no one was happy to see the cause of their misery. I understood why, but it stung. I wanted to spend time with my family in sobriety and decompress after four months of twelve-hour shifts. Instead, it was a time of hurt and frustration for all of us. When I chose drugs over my family I had created a void. We were all struggling to fill that emptiness, each in our own way.

Tiffany was sullen, with little to say. According to Cloudy, she was out of control. Now seventeen, she had been drinking, smoking pot and running wild. As the daughter of an addict, the apple was rotting at the base of the tree. At eleven, Nate had been suspended from school for fighting three times in the past year and now needed to take summer classes to keep up with his peers.

Cloudy was doing her best, but she had been doing it by herself for almost eight years and she was worn down. With a full time job in Portland she had little time for the kids, the house or the property, and of course I was to blame for it all.

They all were uncomfortable around me, and not knowing what else to do, I ripped through thousands of weeds with a gas weed-whacker, split round after round of firewood, and struggled through a few minor home repairs. At night, I walked down the trail to the cabin where Cloudy and I had first twined our lives, and tried to sleep amidst the stench of rat droppings and regret.

Cloudy and I circled each other like cats until the day before my flight back to Alaska. Overcome with remorse and sadness, I finally put my longing into words.

"Cloud, I know how much I've hurt you and the kids and I am so, so sorry. I'd really like to try to make things right with you someday."

"You son-of-a-bitch," she exploded. "Don't you get it? I can't trust you, not ever! I'm letting you be here for the kids but you make my skin crawl! You and I are done and I don't want to talk about it again! Understand?" She stood shaking, her fists clenched. Nate peered from the doorway behind her. Obviously he and Tiffany had heard our exchange.

"All right, I hear you," I said softly. "I'm sorry you feel that way."

It was a relief to leave. Things had gone badly and I was no longer holding out any hope for reconciliation with Cloudy. Tiffany and Nate desperately needed a father and I resolved to call regularly to remind them that I cared.

I climbed down from the Goose on May 31st and managed to grab several hours sleep before returning to the graveyard shift. Later that evening I called Cloudy to let her know I was back.

"Damn it, Doug! Your daughter tried to push me down the stairs last night and I had to call the sheriff. I could have been killed!" Cloudy was in full drama mode and while I was sure there had been a blow up, I knew she sometimes exaggerated. I tried to remain calm.

"So are you all right? Where's Tiffy now?"

"I think I wrenched my back and Tiffany is still here. The deputies put the fear of god into her, but it won't last. I'm signing papers tomorrow with a rep from a drug rehab center in Seattle. I'm going to drive her up there on Saturday. I can't take this anymore."

I was stunned but there was nothing I could do. My presence in Portland hadn't helped at all.

"I'm so sorry this is happening Cloud, but I trust your judgment. I don't see what I can do except keep working. Maybe this is what she needs."

"She needs a father she can count on, why don't you work on that? I don't have the energy for this." I was left holding a dead phone.

In my short absence the days on Akutan had grown noticeably longer and at midnight the remnants of the sunset still lingered over the mountains. A few days later on a short hike I saw how much the island had changed. Summer was in full swing and plants had exploded from the earth. Willows clogged the gullies and bottom land and berry bushes sprinkled the tundra. Even the rocks were covered with new moss and lichen.

In the galley it was as if I'd never left.

"Hey Dodd, sit down and have some of this lousy food. How are things?" Mike was sitting across from Carl as usual and I sat down, feeling like I belonged.

"It's all good, Mike. You're not happy unless you're complaining, are you? Want to hike over to the hot springs with me? I'm gonna find out about those cows, one way or the other."

"No thanks, Dodd, the pushki weed is bad right now."

"What," I glanced at Carl, "is pushki weed?"

"Heracleum maximum," Carl intoned, "also known as cow parsnip, has a hollow stalk that contains a sap which has photosensitive properties. Kind of like a sunburn. The stuff is all over and the leaves get as big as a dinner plate."

"Okay, so how careful do I need to be?"

"Just try not to get the juice on your bare skin and if you do wash it off right away."

"Guess I'll find out pretty soon. First good day I'm going to look for the cows. I saw something last time I was out might have been them, but I was too far away to tell."

"Well," Carl replied, "remember: take pictures."

CHAPTER 32

CATTLE, CONFUSION AND CHANGE

JUNE, 2001 AKUTAN

A few days later, early on a sunny afternoon, I stood, panting and sweaty, on the ridge top looking down into Hot Springs Bay. While I'd been away, the vegetation had gone berserk. The willows were thicker than before and I had fought my way through head-high pushki weeds. I certainly couldn't see any cows and this felt more and more like a fool's errand. Nevertheless, I slid and traversed my way down the slope, plunged into vegetation over my head, and walked in what I hoped was the correct direction.

Without warning, I broke through a screen of willows and found myself facing two cows and a calf. Stunned, I froze. The scene seemed surreal, and the cows looked out of place as though space aliens had whisked them here from a ranch in Wyoming or Montana as a cosmic joke.

I slowly pulled out the disposable camera I'd picked up at the Trident store and snapped a picture. The beasts were indeed polled Herefords, and I counted about twenty adults, a half dozen yearlings and ten or so calves. They looked to be healthy and in good shape, although almost all their heads bore a distinctly roman nose. After perhaps eight or ten bovine generations without new blood, their gene-pool looked a bit shallow. They stared back at me skeptically. Perhaps they were judging my lineage as well. I snapped another picture and as I eased a little closer, one of the cows snorted loudly and the whole herd spooked. They trotted away a few hundred feet and watched me warily.

I left the cows and spent another thirty minutes locating three or four spots where hot water, presumably from the island's volcano, mixed with the creek and formed steaming pools choked with blue green algae. By then it was time to go and I headed back to the plant.

Some days later I approached Fat Frank at the post office, hoping to learn some more history of the herd.

"Hi Frank. I found those cows the other day. They look pretty good and I was wondering if you knew when Charlie Brown brought them here?"

"Yep, Charlie Brown brought 'em." Fat Frank looked at me for what felt like a long time. "It must have been over thirty years."

"Well, was there anyone besides Charlie involved with the cows?" I probed.

"Yeah, his partner Hans Radtke was there," Frank paused, "but he's dead too."

"Anyone else?" I wasn't ready to give up.

"Charlie Brown had a wife." Frank dropped this bombshell with a little smile.

"So," I finally ventured, "is she still around?" I waited, expecting to hear of her demise, but Frank surprised me.

"Maybe. Her name is Joan. Last I heard she worked in Homer for Gold Rush Realty."

"So," I clarified, "the three of them, Charlie and Joan Brown, and their partner Hans brought the cows thirty years ago. Charlie and Hans died and now Joan works in Homer. Is that right?" Fat Charlie just nodded so I thanked him and headed back toward the plant.

Later that evening I called Cloudy for an update on Tiffany's situation.

"Hey, it's me. I called to talk to Nate and see how things are with Tiffany."

"I got her into treatment all right. It's a thirty-five day inpatient program just outside Seattle and costs a bundle. My co-pay will be about $2,500. Thank God your dad sent me a check."

"Any word yet on how she's doing?"

"Nope – no phone calls for at least the first two weeks, maybe longer, it just depends. I did get a letter. She says she's sorry. I hope the treatment works better on her than it did on you." Her sarcasm recalled my countless pathetic apologies and I cringed.

"Is there anything I can do to help?" I braced myself for another outburst.

"Actually, yes. Her counselor suggested that each family member write a letter telling Tiffy how her behavior affected them. I told them about your drug history and they said your letter should be very short. Just tell her you love her and want her to get well. Can you manage that?"

"Sure. Give me the address and I'll send it tomorrow. We should get a plane pretty soon. The weather has been good. How's Nate doing with all this?"

"Who knows? I'll let him tell you himself. Nathan! Get down here, your Dad's on the phone. That boy just doesn't seem to understand that actions have consequences. I'm going to have to find him a therapist who's covered by my insurance. It's late here and I'm a wreck from all this. Here's Nate. Bye."

"Hello son, how are you?"

"Fine." The word dropped flatly in my ear.

"It sounds like you might be having some problems at summer school."

"School sucks and my teachers are stupid."

"I'm sorry to hear that. Is there anything that would make it better?"

"I hate Corbett! I want to go to school in Portland. There's nobody here that looks like me and some of the boys call me names."

"Have you told your mom?"

"She doesn't care. She says it's my fault." I could hear the tears behind his angry words.

"Nate, I'm so sorry I can't be there for you. I haven't been a very good father, but I promise you that will change. I love you. I'll always love you. Try not to get in fights, they just make things worse. I'll call you again next week, okay?"

"Okay."

"Bye, son." I hung up the phone, ashamed to be of so little use, and returned to work in a black mood. Later that same evening – early morning rather – I was standing on a catwalk thinking about change. As I hosed down the sides of first tank, where the raw sewage entered the plant, I remembered my mother's words back on the 3-D.

"The leopard doesn't change his spots, and people just don't change," she would proclaim and Walter would nod agreement. Yet I knew changes occurred every day. For an individual, a marriage, a divorce or the loss of a job can have a lifelong impact.

So, if change was possible, could I change in a positive way? I dragged the hose down the catwalk, away from the worst of the stink, to the next tank where bacteria worked to break down the raw sewage.

Thirty-five years earlier in Missoula, when I started using drugs regularly, my friends and I derided the idea that they could ever create problems for us. The anti-drug propaganda was just a joke, made up by straight people. When I was busted, the laws were stupid. When a friend OD'd we agreed he should have known better. Later in my first stint in treatment someone asked me to name my drug of choice. My reply, 'whatever you've got", was flippant, but the joke was on me.

For years I'd built and polished a shell of sarcastic humor that frustrated my parents. Meanwhile, inside my head, I feared that if people could see the real me they would turn away in disgust. I used drugs to fight those fears, but they always came back sharper and more strident than before.

As I confronted my insecurities without my buffer of drugs or alcohol, I realized that for me there had been no single turning point or event. Hundreds, perhaps thousands of times I chose to make excuses and get high rather than face things about myself that I didn't like. My denial had shifted gradually from "I can quit any time, I just don't want to," to "I'm an addict and I can't quit, so why try?" I had made bad choices and then refused to take responsibility for them. I had cast myself as a victim in my own melodrama for years, and now I was sick of it.

I pulled the hose to the last tank. By the time the raw sewage reached this tank it had been transformed by the addition of various chemicals and gradual bacterial action, into a colorless, almost odorless liquid. Now I would disinfect it with chlorine, neutralize any excess and return the now-pure water to the bay.

What changes might come if I continued to stay clean? I wasn't sure, but when Cloudy had berated me during my recent visit to Oregon I could have gone out and bought crack. I had cash and it would have been easy to score. Instead, for the first time in over thirty years, I hadn't escaped into drugs. Instead I'd spent my money on a used laptop. That was a change.

I now had a year of sobriety. If there had been no single turning point in my disease, maybe the same would hold true of my recovery. One day at a time. Maybe that annoying AA slogan was right:

Standing on the catwalk that night, I found myself laughing aloud. What could be simpler? If sewage could change, so could I! My job was the equivalent of a twelve step treatment program for sewage! I didn't even have to take time off to attend. All I had to do to was follow the rules and be willing to trust a God I wasn't sure existed. There on the catwalk I screamed out the words:

"I give up God. I'm ready, but please? I could use a little help!"

Chapter 33

The Write Stuff for a Miracle

July – August 2001, Akutan

"My name is Doug and I'm an addict."

"Welcome, Doug." Two pairs of eyes, one hazel, the other ice-blue, held me in their grip. The eyes belonged to middle-aged, white males I'd seen around the Trident offices. I was very nervous telling my story to two plant managers.

"I never took a drink or a drug till I was twenty. After that I sort of went crazy. I used pot, booze, and cocaine. I claimed I could quit anytime, but never did. By the time I admitted I had a problem I'd lost my job. Now I'm divorced, my kids hate me, and my friends are gone I'm fifty-five years old. I've been clean for a year and don't want to go back to using. I'm also lonely as hell."

"You're sober today, Doug," ice-blue spoke up sharply, "and that's good, but you have to live with what you did. Some things can't be fixed. You can't blame somebody else for your problem, and if you want to get well you can't feel sorry for yourself, either. You had a family, but after years of screwing things up don't expect forgiveness anytime soon."

"I know this is my fault and I know some things aren't possible. I just feel like I'm waiting for something but I don't know what."

"Sometimes," hazel offered softly, "the only thing to do is just stay clean and keep your head down. Working here can be a real blessing if you take it a day at a time."

"Yes," ice-blue agreed, "if you remember to 'let go and let God' and turn it over you can expect a miracle."

Over the years these AA slogans had always felt hollow but this time was different. That time at the treatment plant, when I shouted to God from the catwalk, had been a Jericho moment. Within the year the walls inside me crumbled.

It all started without fanfare. To keep my mind occupied, I had started writing a few short pieces about the Trident plant, the village and the island itself. I keyed them into my new used laptop and found I enjoyed the experience. When an engineer offered his old dot matrix printer for fifty bucks, I snapped it up along with a few hundred sheets of paper.

After another hike to observe the cows, I decided to include a piece on them in what was becoming a collection. To do that though, I needed more information on their origin. Based on Fat Frank's information, a link to the feral Herefords was the widow Brown.

On July 26th I mailed a short letter of inquiry to the person I had come to think of as the Cow Woman. I mentioned my literary efforts and my history as a Montana rancher – both being a bit of a stretch, considering that I was unpublished and had left the 3-D when I was 23. My contact information was sparse: Joan Brown, Gold Rush Realty, and Homer, Alaska, so I used it all. I obtained the Homer zip code, mailed my letter and waited. What did I have to lose?

To people on Akutan, the Dutch Harbor airport was a postal Bermuda Triangle. Flights in and out were often delayed or canceled due to bad weather, and baggage of all kinds tended to accumulate in the Dutch airport. Sometimes the mail room overflowed, and based on how many damp, bedraggled letters with outdated postmarks I received, some of those bags must have languished in damp corners for weeks.

While I waited, I explored more of the island. On the south side of the bay, almost directly across from the Trident plant, a nameless peak crowded the water's edge. My map showed it to be 1,660 feet high, and in an hour I could walk around the head of the bay to the remains of the old whaling station at the peak's base. From there it was another hour to the top. It was a delightful summer climb, very steep with a couple of short knife edge ridges. The summit offered a panorama of the plant, the village, and the mountains on the island's north side. I climbed the peak three times that summer and always returned to the plant rejuvenated.

At least one evening a week, I called Cloudy, or tried to. Over the din created by five processors shouting simultaneously in Tagalog, Cloudy informed me that not much had changed. Money was tight, Tiffy was nearly done with rehab and Nate was still struggling in school. Nate said little, but at least he knew I was alive.

Whether it was the climbing, the AA meetings or the calls to my family, I had no urge to get high. Alcohol was available in the village at the Roadhouse, but when it was open, I was at work. Some engineers kept bottles in their rooms and probably cocaine as well but I never asked and they never offered.

By mid-August, weeks had passed with no word from the Cow Woman. Planes came and went. Had my letter vanished in a postal black hole? Perhaps the Cow Woman too had passed and I would never know the story of the wild cows. My first letter from Joan Brown, handwritten on two yellow legal-size pages, and dated August 12th, 2001, arrived on the next plane.

The Cow Woman told me she was 68 years old, the winner of several writing contests and a published writer herself. She was considering writing her own memoir covering her five years as a homesteader on Akutan. She possessed "a wealth of information" about the island, the cows and the natives which she would consider sharing with me if I would just answer a few simple questions. Why was I on Akutan? What kind of writing did I do? Had I published anything? She would share – but needed to know "a little more about you first."

I was devastated. I hadn't even considered that I might have to reveal details of my past. I was so stupid. Of course she would want to know more about this impudent interloper trying to push his way into her life. I could lie – invent a past free from drug addiction and criminal behavior – or I could tell the truth and risk never hearing from her again. There was no middle ground.

My first inclination was to lie. I had lied to my parents about believing in their Baptist God and about smoking pot. I had lied to girlfriends about my devotion, and to my probation officer about my repentance. My escape from Montana and subsequent reinvention of myself in Portland was one big lie. I'd polished my prevarications at the Water Bureau and mastered mendacity during my marriage to Cloudy. I lied for fun, to get high, for practice and out of desperation created by previous falsehoods.

I was tired of keeping track of my lies. It seemed to me that the Cow Woman's five years as a homesteader on this inhospitable rock entitled her to the truth. I surrendered my fears and answered her questions as honestly as I could.

Chapter 34

Fools Rush In

September – December, 2001

What followed, whether coincidence or divine plan, resembled a clichéd Hollywood screenplay. Joan and I exchanged pictures and letters. Each plane in or out of Akutan carried at least one, and sometimes two or three. Joan had been widowed for two years and didn't enjoy being alone. Our interests overlapped nicely from music, to books, to our love of the island. Even more amazing, she did not reject me because of my addiction. If two lonely strangers correspond enough, something is bound to happen. By Thanksgiving, I was in love.

Around December 1, Trident finished hooking up landlines in their four bunkhouses and I now had a working phone in my room. Joan had enclosed her number in one of her letters and I decided to call. The person who picked up sounded girlish - like a teenager with a faint Midwestern accent – and at first I thought I'd misdialed. That proved false and our first conversation was full of promise.

With daily phone calls, our flood of letters abated. Joan and I talked for hours. I told her I had already made plans to spend Christmas in Portland with my kids. I told her I wanted to visit her in Homer before returning to Akutan and that by May I hoped to be done with Trident for good. Then, if she was willing, we could get married. Ultimately, she agreed.

I was filled, first with excitement, and then frustration. I had great news and no one to share it with. Few families or friendships are strong enough to weather thirty years of drug abuse. My family had shrunk to Walter, my sister, and Cloudy and the kids. Besides Kermit, Carol and the Wolffs, I had retained one old friend, Mike Parsons, from the water bureau.

In December I wrote a letter describing the cows, my frustrating search for the Cow Woman and its strange and wonderful culmination. I sent copies to friends and family, including Cloudy.

I called Cloudy from the Seattle train station on December 21. It was Friday and my flight out of Dutch had been delayed by a storm. “You were supposed to be here yesterday, Doug. I can’t rely on anything you say, can I?” Her voice snapped and I pulled the phone back from my ear involuntarily.

“I was stuck overnight in Dutch Harbor because of weather. I told you this might happen.”

“Whatever. You can sleep on the couch tonight but you need to find some other place to stay and you can take Tiffy with you. I’ve had it with her.”

“Okay, I was hoping to use the cabin. What’s up with Tiffany?”

“Everything’s iced up in the cabin. Your daughter’s not using yet but she’s being a total bitch. She fights with Nate all the time and I need a break.” She sighed heavily.

“I’ll get to Portland in about five and a half hours. Will you be able to meet my train?”

“That won’t be convenient.” Her words hung in the air like wet laundry frozen on a line.

After she hung up, I called Mike Parsons. I'd feared something like this might happen and had already asked him if there was any way he could put me up for a few days. He had agreed without question and now I needed to alert him to my arrival. Mike said the offer was still open and told me he would pick me up at the station. I left a message for Cloudy, telling her I would be spending the night at Mike's. It was good to visit with him and his family again, but after dinner, I began to fade.

"I'm really beat, Mike. I left Akutan yesterday morning and it's catching up with me. I'll call Cloudy in the morning. Maybe she'll change her mind and let me stay there."

"Whatever works for you. Either way is fine," Mike said.

When I called Cloudy the next morning, she proposed what amounted to a cease-fire. I could sleep on her couch. The kids and I would cut and decorate a tree. She would cook and we would celebrate Christmas. I was stunned. What followed was not 'the best Christmas ever'. Cloudy and Tiffany weren't speaking, and Tiffany told me she'd spent a night in jail when Cloudy called the sheriff during an argument that got physical. I could take no more.

"This has to stop. Tiffany, we've got to get you out of here."

"I can't stand it here anymore with her and Nate. She says she's glad I'm in recovery, but it's really hard to get to meetings. She doesn't want me driving her pickup at night, and she expects me to come home right after school, fix dinner and be responsible for Nate. Of course he won't do anything I tell him."

"Do you have money for a place?"

"No, but I've been looking for a job. I'll probably have to quit school." Tiffany had just earned a 4.0 for her first semester of classes at the local community college and I wanted her to remain enrolled.

"You may not have to do that. The college fund we set up pays for books and tuition, right?" At her nod I continued. "If you could find a place within biking distance from the school you wouldn't need the pickup. Then, if you could get a part time job, maybe you could go to school and meetings and still be able to pay your rent."

"Yeah, but even with a job it would take me months to save up the money for a place."

"Haven't we always told you not to worry about the 'yeah-buts'?" I smiled. "I'll help you for the first few months with the rent, how about that?"

"Oh, Dad!" She seemed stunned or perhaps doubtful. "Don't say that if you don't mean it."

"Tiffy, I can't change who I was, but I'm not that person any more. If you want, I'll help you find a place and move in. I'll pay the deposit and rent until you find a part time job."

"Will you tell Mom?"

"We'll tell her together."

And so we did. Two days later, after considering and rejecting half dozen places as either too expensive or too disgusting, we found a small studio in downtown Gresham for $500 a month, utilities included. The landlady was skeptical since Tiffany was just eighteen and unemployed, but when I offered $1,500 up front to cover first and last month's rent and a damage deposit, she took the money.

That may have marked the moment Tiffany began to accept that I had changed. Over the next several years she gradually forgave me for the pain I had inflicted, but this was a beginning.

Most evenings during my visit, after Cloudy and the kids were asleep, I called Joan and we whispered reassurances to each other. We could hardly wait to meet face to face.

Early Wednesday morning January 2, Cloudy brought up money, something I should have been expecting.

"If you do end up marrying that woman I'm concerned about the kids. You still owe me over $50,000 in back child support. How are you going to afford that and your regular payments? Are you going to keep working at Trident? Where is all that money going to come from?"

"I'm planning to go back to Trident for a while, you'll keep getting child support," I assured her.

"Okay, but what if you die? I want the kids to have money for college," she persisted.

"So what do you want me to do? I fly to Alaska tomorrow night."

"We could run down to Salem and talk to the people at PERS; hear what they have to say."

Three hours later we were inside the Public Employee Retirement System building, sitting in hard chairs, listening to soft music and waiting. When we walked out an hour later, it was done, carved in bureaucratic stone. I would start drawing my retirement immediately, and if I died before Cloudy, she would receive about $25,000 per year, for the rest of her life. Joan would get nothing. If I hadn't been hungry, tired and guilt ridden I might have balked at the deal. It became a moot point and I hoped I wouldn't be sorry.

Chapter 35

A Homer Surprise

January 2002, Homer, Alaska

The heater in the half-full plane was struggling and the other passengers and I sat hunched against the January cold. The man seated just behind me had fallen asleep on takeoff and his snoring, combined with the sneezing of a pudgy fellow across the aisle, and formed a duet that competed with the engine's drone. The flight to Homer lasted barely a half hour, but was still long enough for my imagination to go crazy. So much could go wrong when Joan and I finally met in person. What if all our little quirks and nuances – the things that make every human unique – simply didn't mesh? What if one of us found the other physically repugnant? Maybe we were fools, doomed to mutual disappointment.

Realistically, I didn't have much to offer a partner besides a history of lies and a mountain of debts. I'd confessed to having had an addiction, but held back some of the most graphic details. If I told Joan I'd smoked crack for fifteen years and been clean for less than two, would I be on the next plane out of town?

I scrunched down and peered out the scratched, Plexiglas window. I could see the flash of the setting sun on water, but where was the airport or, for that matter, the town? As we banked, I glimpsed a boney finger of land that reached out in the bay as though pointing at jagged, snow topped peaks. I dipped my head for a better look, but we turned again and my view shifted to roads and buildings.

I'd heard of Homer before I came to Alaska. After my mother divorced him, Bob had remarried and in 1969 relocated to Alaska, first to Anchorage, then to Homer. Bob fathered two more children, a boy and a girl, who both lived in Homer, a village with less than 4,000 residents. It seemed beyond bizarre that I had fallen in love with a woman I'd never seen, who lived in the same tiny town as my two half-siblings who I barely knew.

The plane landed and taxied to the terminal. As the engines died, the flight attendant popped the door and lowered the steps. We stood, stooping in the low cave-like cabin, and shuffled forward. I slipped in between Sneezy and Sleepy and stifled a nervous impulse to break into song. 'Hi ho, hi ho, it's off to work we go'. Outside my breath steamed as we trudged toward the terminal.

Inside, Snow White waited. We embraced. She was just right - Goldilocks with dark hair. Cinderella drove a Dodge and I could see my future in her eyes. Her castle was only a little larger than my bunkhouse suite, but it held all that mattered and her kisses ensorcelled me. The next few days were a joy. Best of all, after I bared my past life Joan stunned me by declaring that she still wanted me for a partner – warts and all.

Although I had planned to work another season at Trident, I changed my mind after just a week in Homer with my new love. Together, we decided that I would return to Akutan for no more than a month so I could train my replacement. I owed them that much. I had already started withdrawing my pension, so

I would have money coming in. Once done with Trident, Joan and I would drive down the Alcan so she could meet my family. Then, around the end of June, we'd drive back to Homer to get married.

That final month on Akutan while I was training my replacement, I thought about how close I'd come to losing everything. During my drugging I lied, stole and broke promise after promise. I needed to make what amends I could. I was off to a good start with Tiffany but to regain the trust of Nathan and my father I would need time. I decided to take responsibility and be completely honest about my many mistakes. The first step would require a visit to Missoula.

Chapter 36

Facing the Elephant with Walter and Leola

April 2002 Missoula

When I took Joan to meet Walter I didn't know what to expect. After Mom died, Dad had retired, sold the 3-D, and married a widow, Leola Masters, all in one year. By 2002 they had bought a small house on a half-acre in Missoula. I'd already met Lee and paid them one previous visit, but the gap between Dad and me felt as wide as ever. Our conversations seldom moved beyond the weather and the economy. We never discussed Mom, my childhood on the ranch or his experiences in the War. My addiction was the elephant in the room – never mentioned, always there.

"Good morning. Did you sleep okay?" Lee smiled from the stove as I walked into the room. "The coffee's a little strong this morning. Walter's out in the yard with the dog."

"Thanks, I could sure use a cup. Yesterday was a long day. I guess the trip finally caught up with me." We'd got in at nine the night before, after driving all the way from Edmonton, and gone straight to bed. Now it was 7:30 and from the looks of the kitchen, Lee had been busy. The table was set for four with place mats and cloth napkins. I sipped the coffee, hot and black, just the way Joan and I liked it. "This is good; I'll take Joan a cup. She'll be out as soon as she gets her face on." When I returned Lee continued.

"We have bacon and eggs, pancakes and some of the peaches Walter and I canned last year. I hope that's okay." I watched Lee bustle about the kitchen. Short, slim and energetic, she darted about from stove to refrigerator to table. She seemed nearly as active as Joan, though I knew that at nearly eighty she was twelve years older.

"It sounds great, Lee. You've really gone to a lot of trouble."

"It's no trouble. Your dad likes a good breakfast and I enjoy fixing it. We're both so pleased to see you and meet Joan."

"Well thanks, we're happy to be here." I refilled my cup. "I'll step out in the yard and see what Dad is up to."

From the back door I could see him over by a large fir where the dog had something on the ground.

"Morning, Dad. What's going on?"

"Good morning, Douglas. Tess just got a squirrel. As soon as she's done with it I'll put it in the trash. Lee will be glad to know she caught another one."

"Do you guys have a war on squirrels?"

"They get in the bird feeder. Lee and I really like to watch the birds but those darn squirrels are just like rats. Tess is a good dog."

Tess, a compact black and brown Shepard mix, looked up at her name, gave her prey a final shake and charged across the yard to the fence barking.

A boy on a bicycle rode by. "Tess, that's enough," Walter commanded without much enthusiasm. She ignored him. "Tess!" His tone was sharp and Tess quieted at once. "She's a good watchdog," he said, and I thought of the ranch where a good watchdog was valued as the first line of defense against bears and coyotes. Dad's body might be in the city, but his heart still roamed.

"We better go in, I'm sure Lee has breakfast ready," he said.

Back in the kitchen, Lee and Joan were chatting like old friends. I had been apprehensive about the whole visit, mainly because of my history, but also because I wondered how Joan and Lee would get on. So far, that at least didn't seem to be a problem. I was still uneasy about talking with Dad. Would I be able to find the words to express my regret for what I had done? Would I feel any closer to this man I respected but didn't understand?

Breakfast was, of course, excellent, if a bit more than I'd needed. Afterward, Dad and I sat in the living room while the women finished up in the kitchen. It was a very traditional arrangement and not Joan's style, but as I had learned, she was a polite person and didn't fuss. I knew I would hear from her later, in private.

As Dad and I sat looking at each other, small talk suddenly seemed impossible.

"Oh Dad, I've thought about this every day on the island. I'm sorry for all the things I did over the years." My voice broke and I couldn't go on. "Dad, I am so, so sorry."

"There'll be time for that later, Douglas. I want to hear all about your trip." I brushed my eyes with my sleeve as Lee and Joan walked into the living room. I described our drive from Homer. Joan explained our wedding plans, but other than that said little. Dad and Lee seemed interested.

"Would you and Joan like to take a drive up Snow Bowl," Dad asked? "We could come down that old cat road from the saddle. We'd need to take the pickup."

"I'd like that." I replied.

"Cat road?" Joan queried. "I don't like narrow roads, especially if there's a drop off."

"Well you might not like this road then. Don't worry though, it's perfectly safe," Dad explained.

"I won't worry because I won't be there! You men go ahead; I'll stay here with Lee." Joan stepped into the guest room and shut the door.

"She's a woman who knows her own mind," Dad laughed, "I guess that's a good thing."

"Yup, that's for sure. With Joan I always know where I stand."

Dad handed me a set of keys. In the past he had always done the driving and it felt funny to be behind the wheel of his white F-150. Tess jumped in beside Dad and we were off.

I drove under the freeway and headed up Grant Creek through a housing development. All my old landmarks were gone and I didn't recognize anything.

Farther along, Dad pointed into the trees above the road. "Up there you can see where we had that arson fire in 79."

"You sent me a clipping about that. Did they ever find out who started it?"

"Pretty sure it was a local kid with fireworks but his father was a lawyer so nothing ever came of it. We lost about a hundred acres of timber. Your mother was so sick by then that I didn't even tell her about it. I almost logged that area the year before and decided not to. That was a mistake." He shook his head. "Probably lost forty or fifty thousand when that stand of ponderosa pine went up."

"Dad, mistakes are the story of my life. The fire was just bad luck; there was no way you could have known. The stuff I did hurt so many people – you and Mom, then, later, Cloudy and the kids. In AA they talk about making amends. Well, it's too late to fix things between Mom and me, and I don't know yet about the kids and Cloudy."

Dad stayed silent and I drove on. The road climbed through a series of switchbacks and narrowed to a single lane with pull-outs. At the ridge marking the drainage between Grant and Butler Creeks, Dad pointed to the left.

"That's it and the gate's open," he said.

I shifted into four-wheel-drive and turned onto a narrow track that descended into the Butler Creek drainage. We were now on what used to be the 3-D. We were technically trespassing, but I felt like I was coming home.

That feeling vanished five minutes later as we broke out of the trees onto the flat next to what had been the turkey pen. All the fences and corrals had been eradicated and the sheep barn, chicken houses, granary and machine sheds were gone as well.

Butler Creek itself was invisible, completely overgrown by willows and brush. The cat track we'd followed down from the ridge became a street and we were suddenly on 'Dodd Lane'.

"This is weird, Dad. It's like they got rid of everything."

"Almost. They left the two houses, rented them out. But you can see the people in them don't take care of anything," Dad snorted. "That's not the worst," he continued. "Remember the rock walls? Well, they ripped them all down and sold the rocks to a landscaper. Four generations of Chilcotes and Dodds worked for ninety years on this miserable place, and for what? So some developer could cut it up into forty-acre tracts, put up McMansions and sell them for half a million each.? Every lot is pie shaped. That way they can all claim creek frontage, even if it's only a few feet."

I'd never heard Dad talk like this, angry and hurt at the same time. I turned off Dodd Lane onto Butler Drive and drove through a field where I had bucked hay in the summer and sledded in the winter - the same field where Dad had rolled the tractor. I began to see houses, sprinkled across the hills, tucked into the timber. They looked expensive and out of place. The owners would have nice views. By now it was almost noon on a sunny Saturday, but I didn't see any people. No children playing, no walkers or bicyclists. The houses could have been abandoned.

"Strange," I reflected, "there's no sign of life. I've walked all over these hills, shot gophers above that meadow and followed milk cows down that trail. I wonder if these people ever go outside. Maybe they just come here to sleep."

I parked next to the road in what used to be our upper meadow, rolled down the window and cut the engine. I could smell the alfalfa and hear the grasshoppers. Dad opened his door and Tess hopped to the ground and began investigating.

"When I was little I loved this place. Later I hated it. Now I miss it. Growing up, I didn't think you even wanted Nancy and me here."

"You and Nancy were one of the main reasons I asked Jerry to marry me. I contracted mumps in my late teens and couldn't have kids of my own. Jerry and I made a lot of mistakes. You don't know this, but you were such an angry child I thought then you needed some help – I even found a counselor – but Jerry wouldn't allow it."

"Did she ever say why?"

"No, but I think there were two reasons. First, she was ashamed." Dad sighed. "To her, having emotional problems was as bad as getting divorced. She worried about what people would say. The other thing, the counselor was a man and after the way Bob treated her she didn't trust men. She never got over that. When she was dying I found out she didn't even trust me."

"You can't know that, Dad. After everything you did for her that doesn't make sense."

"It's true though. A couple weeks before she died, during one of her lucid spells, she said she wanted me to promise something. 'Promise me you'll take care of my kids,' she said. She didn't need to ask me to do that! That really hurt. You and

Nancy were always mine. How could she not know that?" He had never spoken to me like this.

"What I did wasn't your fault, Dad. I was lucky to have you for a father instead of Bob, but I was too angry and selfish to appreciate it."

"I had my own problems, Douglas. Still do. You know why I didn't talk about the war? I had nightmares for sixty years and talking just made it worse. I didn't think there was anything I could do about it. Lee got me to see a doctor. He says I have PTSD from the war and that it caused the dreams. He uses neuro-feedback. Jerry wouldn't have approved, but it helps a lot.

"How does it work?"

"Darned if I know." Dad laughed and shook his head. "He hooks me up to some electrodes. Then we just talk. It shouldn't work, but it does."

"That's great, Dad, I'm glad it's helping. That reminds me, when Mom was dying she told me that when Bob broke up with her, his girlfriend was right there with him. That really embarrassed her and I think she had some PTSD of her own. Both of you needed help. Anyway, I would have been a handful under the best of circumstances."

"I always wanted you to become a lawyer. I thought you had the mind for it. I just wasn't smart enough to raise you right."

"There was nothing you could have done. I lied because I had really low self-esteem and once I started I couldn't stop. Can you understand that?"

"I think so," he spoke slowly. "People get trapped by their lies, but lies only work if somebody believes them, and in the end nobody believed you."

"Yes! That's it exactly! That's why working for the Wolffs was important. They didn't know about my lies and when they gave me a chance I didn't lie to them. It was like a fresh start. I know that was when I first stopped lying."

We sat, silent for a while, listening to the birds and the occasional whistle of a gopher. I closed my eyes, inhaled deeply and let the smells of alfalfa and clover take me back to the ranch. A roar of engines jerked me out of my reverie and two dirt bikes blew by us, trailing a cloud of choking dust.

"Tess, get over here! We better get back or they'll eat without us," Dad laughed. Tess jumped into his lap and I started the truck.

Our talk was a huge relief but Dad was still reluctant to discuss his feelings. Fortunately Lee and Dad connected with Joan and her open, direct manner in a way they never had with Cloudy and his last remark before Joan and I hit the road for Portland was especially telling.

"Douglas, I'm happy you finally found a good woman, one you're really compatible with."

Chapter 37

Ammends, Where Possible (Hard Times, Come Again No More.)

May 2002 to 2004, Portland and Homer

Compared to what followed, reconciliation with Walter had been a cakewalk. I wanted back in Nate's and Tiffany's lives but unless Cloudy cooperated it might be impossible. We had divorced more than eight years before and I had naively assumed that when a marriage dissolved each party gave up the right to dictate to the other. When I called Cloudy in April to tell her that Joan and I planned to marry that summer and settle in Portland, she objected.

"I think you should wait a couple years. You hardly know this woman. Have you told her about your history?"

"She knows I used drugs and how I screwed up. I'm not that person any more. I've been clean almost two years now." I replied.

"That's what you say. I can't believe any decent woman would marry you if she knew the things you've done," she shot back. "I don't want you in Portland. Word will get out that you're back and that will reflect on me. I don't want you ruining my reputation."

"Excuse me, somebody's at the door, I'll call you back." This was a lie, but I had to get off the phone before I started screaming. Her words sounded insane. There were two million people in greater Portland and she was telling me I couldn't live there? With my memories, Portland was the last place I *wanted* to live but I felt a strong need to reconcile with my children, especially Nate. When I related Cloudy's words to Joan I expected she would want to return to Homer rather than face such a hostile situation. I was wrong.

"She's not the boss of me!" Joan said vehemently, and we went ahead with our plans.

When Joan and I arrived in Portland in May, Cloudy and Nate were at loggerheads. He faced suspension from school and Cloudy grudgingly accepted my presence, but with conditions. While Joan and I were still getting settled, she emailed me a set of demands: I must submit to weekly drug tests with the results being sent to her. Joan could not set foot on Cloudy's property, and she would not speak to Joan. I would deal with Nate's problems at school and any further contact with Nate would be entirely at her discretion. All this was hard for me to accept but in nearly every way, Cloudy held the cards.

The divorce settlement gave her sole custody and set basic child support at $1,100 a month with a couple hundred more going toward back support. I hadn't missed a payment since I started working at Akutan, but I owed a bundle for arrears. If I went to court against Cloudy, I would surely lose.

Only one factor worked in my favor and it was painfully ironic. Cloudy and Nate were like water and sodium; brought too close together, they exploded. After Nate turned twelve, those explosions became more violent. They needed the time apart that my presence provided. Nate shuttled between Cloudy's twenty acres outside of town and my rental in Portland. There was no regular schedule. Sometimes Cloudy would call and then, arrive an hour later with a sullen Nate who might stay for four hours or four days.

At that time Nate was attending Beaumont, a crowded, racially mixed middle school in northeast Portland. To my eyes, Nate and the other boys of color looked like gangsta wannabes, with their do-rags, too-big pants sagging halfway to their knees, and "Yo, Wassup Dawwg?" greetings. I watched the white kids see him as 'black' and the black kids as 'not black enough'. Nate and I both hated Beaumont and though he graduated, I can't say he learned much.

Nate's next school year was worse and by the spring of 2003 he was skipping school and running away. He was thirteen, and out of desperation Cloudy and I sent him to the Flying J, a Christian boy's ranch in central Washington State. The staff seemed decent, if very conservative, and Nate got to build a go-kart in their shop, something he thoroughly enjoyed. The Flying J cost over three grand a month and I paid half. I was also paying over $1,400 each month in child support, current and back, at the same time. In one year child support and the Flying J cost me over $35,000. I had my pension and a delivery job, while Joan, now seventy, worked as a substitute teacher in the Portland school system. We were still just getting by.

Then in the spring of 2004, with Nate at the Flying J, Cloudy's attorney filed a complicated claim with the state of Oregon for an additional $13,000 in back interest on the child support I owed her. The state approved the claim and there was no way for me to appeal. After spending half my income on my debt for two years, I suddenly owed more than before. As my mom might have phrased it, I was so angry I could spit. After I calmed down, I called Dad.

"Hey Dad, is this a good time to talk?"

"Good morning, Douglas, I was just watching Tess kill another of those miserable squirrels. The young ones are so dumb they've been keeping her busy. How are things in Portland?"

"We're okay. Joan's homesick for Alaska, though. How are you and Lee?"

"Pretty good. I think she might even make me a cherry pie this afternoon."

"Joan made a pie yesterday. Boy, you and I are sure lucky. Hey Dad, I'm calling because I could use some help." I explained that Cloudy had filed a new claim and finished with: "Could you loan me $13,000?" Dad never bad-mouthed anyone but he understood my struggles with Cloudy and I could hear his voice harden.

"How much do you owe altogether?"

"I paid the arrears down from $50,000 to $42,000 over the last year and a half but now they've added another thirteen thousand. I didn't think that was even legal, but they did it." I explained.

"That's gouging. I can help you and it won't be a loan. You know when I sold the ranch I got almost a million dollars? Well, I invested it and I've done okay. I've set up a living trust for you and your sister and I'll just take this out of your share. Get me the total and I'll get a cashier's check for it all. "

"Gosh Dad, I don't expect you to do that. Are you sure?"

"Yes. I don't need the money and I don't like to see you owing that woman anything. You worked on the ranch for years for no pay. Besides, you'll get it anyway when I die."

I thanked him again and that was settled. Although I continued to pay child support for several more years, I was happy to do so and never missed a payment.

Writing about this incident over a dozen years later, I cannot recreate the anger I felt. Forgiveness can be a long, difficult process, but for me, harboring grudges is even harder. No amount of money could erase the pain I had caused Cloudy, and a casual observer, seeing Cloudy and I at our daughter's wedding in 2016, might have mistaken us for friends. At that wedding, Cloudy even spoke to Joan.

Chapter 38

The Best of Times

2004 to 2008 Homer

"Guess what, Doug, I bought us a place!" When the phone rang that May morning I saw it was Joan calling from Homer. We wanted to move back to Homer and the lease on our Portland apartment was almost up, so Joan had flown north before me to look for a house. Nate's year at the Flying J would end in late June and Joan and I were hoping that Nate had matured enough to enjoy a summer with us. Cloudy had agreed as long as Nate returned to Portland in the fall for high school. I had never bought a house and Cloudy had not added me as a co-owner on her property. Rentals didn't count, Joan said, so this would be my first property

"Wow, that's great, Hon. What kind of a house?"

"It's a double wide fixer-upper with three bedrooms and two baths, so Nate can have his own room. It's on four acres, seven miles out East End Road. There's a creek and lots of trees."

"That sounds great. I can hardly wait to get out of Portland."

"How soon can you get here? I miss you," Joan said.

"I miss you too. Give me two weeks."

It took me ten days, not counting the five days I spent on the road, and Nate flew in a week later. Joan had been a Realtor for nineteen years, so I was comfortable having her select a place without my presence. She did not disappoint. The view of the mountains and glaciers across the bay was fantastic. The creek ran east to west through the property, with the trailer sitting to the south on about an acre of flat ground. Our land north of the creek was on a slope, thick with devil's club, elderberry bushes and pushki weeds. There had been some erosion during a spring runoff and the owners had been ready to sell.

The trailer needed a few repairs, but Joan had negotiated an excellent deal and I wasn't worried. The roof and the plumbing had minor leaks. The old furnace didn't work, and the stand supporting the fuel oil tank had to be replaced. Tar and plastic pipe soon fixed the leaks and I ripped out the furnace and installed a Toyo stove. All this took less than a month.

Next I built a greenhouse out of scrap lumber, pallets, used Visqueen and an old screen door. Joan filled the greenhouse with plants, the oven with pies, and covered canvas after canvas with brightly colored oil paintings of landscapes and still lifes.

Nate arrived and he and I stabilized the creek banks and installed a sump pump for irrigation. Then we raked and seeded the rest of the yard, and planted trees and shrubs. Across the creek, I cut hiking trails up the hill where I saw moose, bear and porcupine.

Nate didn't cause any real problems that summer, but he showed little interest in Homer. Joan had a grandson about Nate's age, and I took the two of them across the bay where we hiked a couple miles to a lake. The lake was fed by a melting glacier and contained floating icebergs. It was very popular with tourists but Nate was unimpressed.

Back in Portland, school did not go well for Nate and the time he spent on the Flying J seemed wasted. In 2006 Cloudy sent him back to stay with us in Homer. By then I could tell he was smoking pot. Distracted and sullen, he clashed with Joan immediately. When he quit school, I promised him that if he got his GED and found a job I would help him rent a place. He did both so I kept my promise. Nate continued to use drugs and alcohol, and was soon arrested. After some time in juvenile detention, a judge allowed him to enter rehab in Washington.

Nothing seemed to help. Like me, he had to find his own low bottom. All I could do was watch, hope, love him and try to help. The other details of Nate's story are his own to tell and today he is sober; a responsible and loving father, and my son of whom I am very proud.

In 2007 we sold the trailer and bought a small house in downtown Homer. My pension was enough for us to look for a second home in Montana where we could be close to Dad and Lee, and be only a ten hour drive from Tiffany in Portland. We found a tenant for our Homer house, came to Montana, and started house hunting.

On April 1, 2008, a Tuesday, we signed papers on a beautiful cedar-sided home in Florence, Montana, about twenty miles south of Missoula. At that point, I had been clean over seven years. I had paid off all my back debts and built some savings. I didn't have health insurance but I felt fine. In the words of philosopher A.E. Newman, "What, me worry?"

Chapter 39

Cancer and Empathy

2008 to 2011 Missoula, Alaska, California

The day after we closed on the Florence house, as Joan and I celebrated in a Missoula restaurant, blood suddenly gushed from my nose and dripped onto my plate. Seven days later, after a flurry of tests, Doc Braby, an ENT surgeon removed a malignant tumor the size of a small mouse which had been creeping toward my brain. I was left with a permanently enlarged sinus cavity and $26,000 in medical bills.

Because I had no health insurance, every provider was anxious to be paid. They offered discounts, ranging from ten to twenty percent, for prompt payment in full. I paid out of savings and was healing nicely, when an oncologist insisted I needed radiation.

"I don't see why I need any more treatment. Braby said he got it all." I complained to Joan.

"He said he *thinks* he got everything," she replied. "If he missed just one or two cells they can start to regrow. Trust me, I went through this with Charlie and it's not worth the risk."

Joan's first husband had died of cancer in 1999 and she had cared for him to the end.

"We have two house payments and our savings are trashed. We can't afford more treatment."

"We can if we put a tenant in the Florence house and move back to Homer. You can get your treatments in Anchorage and stay with my son, Malcolm. He's alone in that great big house so there's plenty of room."

I'd learned the futility of arguing with Joan, especially when she was right. We rented out the Florence house and drove up the Alcan. I finished treatment the end of August with radiation burns in my mouth and throat, but finally it was over. I set up a payment plan for the huge bill.

One month later, I was diagnosed with prostate cancer. My birth parents, Jerry and Bob, had both died from cancer, so I shouldn't have been surprised. When I told my urologist, Dr. Turner, that I had no insurance and still owed $65,000 for the radiation treatments, he explained that most prostate cancers are slow growing and suggested I watch and wait for a while. No cutting, no radiation, and no drugs, just wait and monitor. I agreed.

While I waited, I researched alternative treatments. I became a pisca-vegetarian, eliminated most sugar from my diet, and added a tincture concocted by an herbalist in Oregon. These changes, together with a literal handful of other supplements, became my daily routine as I waited on my cancer.

Once I decided to wait, I became more attuned to the needs of other people in Homer. I remembered all the help I had received from the Wolffs, the Jacobsons, and the Mission. I remembered words from an old gospel song: *Why don't you live so God can use you?* - and knew I needed to do something.

Although some local boosters proudly refer to it as "the cosmic hamlet by the sea," Homer, like most small Alaskan towns, has its share of domestic abuse, alcoholism, and drug addiction. The town depends on tourism and fishing, two seasonal and weather dependent jobs, and in a bad year, some residents struggle to put food on the table.

In 2008 I began working at the local food pantry most Mondays. My duties were simple – set up tables, stack cans and sort vegetables, and I became a regular volunteer. I noticed and that some clients appeared to be homeless and many had physical disabilities. Clearly, they had additional needs. Because of my personal history the pantry director asked me to work with clients whose needs went beyond food. When I did, I met people who looked a lot like I had ten years before. It was emotionally difficult work, but I felt useful.

Through 2009, while I watched my cancer and worked at the food pantry, Lee's heart began to fail. Dad agonized as she grew sicker. The doctors tried several treatments, but nothing helped and Lee slept most of the time. Finally, on March 15, 2010, a month after her ninetieth birthday, Lee was gone.

Dad had already buried his parents, a younger brother and my mother. Physically he was strong, but Lee had been the love of his life and emotionally he was in a deep depression. My sister Nancy moved in and with the encouragement of other family members helped him carry on.

In the spring of 2011, six months after I became eligible for medicare, I applied for proton beam radiation treatment at Loma Linda University Medical Center outside Los Angeles. I was accepted and on September 28, I scraped the frost of our windshield, and Joan and I pulled out of Homer. On October 12, we drove into Loma Linda with our air conditioner on.

At Loma Linda I was frustrated at first. The doctors required a second biopsy since it had been three years since my last one. They told me to stop all my alternative treatments. I was anxious and short tempered and I knew it. For three years I had managed my medical treatment and made all the decisions. When I entered Loma Linda, I put my life in their hands.

Thinking back four decades, I remembered my mother's words when she had been ill.

"I don't know whether to laugh or cry so I might as well laugh." Sadly, although she used the expression, I seldom heard her laugh about it. At Loma Linda, the laughing was easy.

The laughter started with Doctor Martel, who monitored my case and met with me privately once a week. He had a Groucho Marx moustache and an apparently endless store of bad jokes.

"How're you doing, Doug? Any problems?"

"No, Doc, I'm fine." Once I got over myself, I was always fine at Loma Linda.

"Okay, I got one for you. This guy gets a complete physical and afterwards the doctor comes in and says to him: 'Sir, I've got two pieces of bad news. First, you have inoperable stage four-cancer and there's nothing I can do.'

'What's the other bad news?' the guy asks.

'You've also got Alzheimer's.'

'Wow!' the patient says, 'well, it could be worse; at least I don't have cancer.'"

After a few of my forty-five proton treatments, I concluded that besides Dr. Martel, the entire department was composed of aspiring comedians. Before every treatment, a patient had to hike up his open-at-the-back gown, and lie on his side so the techs could insert a rectal balloon. This they filled with water, allegedly to prevent radiation damage to the colon. Personally, I suspected they had invented this indignity as a way to perfect their stand-up routines.

"How are ya' today, Doug?" Cindy was perky and looked to be in her mid-twenties.

"Good. This is number eleven."

"So," Cindy's crony, Dave, chimed in, "you know the hospital motto is 'to make man whole,' right?" Dave, who was about Cindy's age, kept his expression serious.

"Un...yeah?" I replied, wondering where this was going.

"Well, each department has its own individual motto. Ours," Cindy smiled proudly, "is to make man's hole bigger." She gave Dave a high five and they both cracked up.

"Believe me, you guys are doing a fine job," I said, joining in their laughter.

Despite their frivolity, the staff seemed very sensitive to each patient's moods. If a man became depressed or angry, the jokes disappeared. For me, the jokes scoured away any scraps of fear that might have existed, and I was grateful for their silly banter.

My treatment continued, five days a week through November and into late December. My final treatment was early the morning of the twenty-third and Joan and I were past ready to go home. By that evening we were at her sister Mary's place in Eloy, Arizona, where we parked our car for the winter. On Christmas Eve, Mary drove us to the Tucson airport and the afternoon of Christmas Day we arrived in Homer. In the six subsequent years neither cancer has reoccurred.

Chapter 40

Hello Dad, and Goodbye

2011 – 2016 Homer and Missoula

In 1970, when I fled Montana, I stopped keeping in touch with my folks. After 2002, when I brought Joan to meet Lee and Dad, I started calling him, usually on Saturday mornings. At first our conversations, separated by 3,000 miles, were awkward. The weather and his garden were safe topics; which of his friends had died since we last spoke was somewhat less so. At the end of each conversation, he would thank me for calling. When I told him I loved him, there would be a silence, then a goodbye.

The calls themselves varied a lot. Sometimes we said hello and not much more, other times we talked for an hour. After Lee died, I began to ask more questions about his life on the ranch, his relationship with his parents and with my mother. Gradually he began to open up.

"I hauled five gallon buckets of water that whole summer." We were talking about the summer of 1931, his first on the ranch. His mother, Myrtle, had just taken ownership. Her mother had died in April and none of Myrtle's sibs were willing to tackle the place in its ruinous condition.

"So you were a water boy at twelve? That must have been hard work." This story was new to me and I wanted to keep him talking.

"All our water came from the creek, and we needed a lot. I must have made fifty trips a day, a bucket in each hand."

"How did you feel about that?" I asked.

"I was her slave." His sharp tone shocked me. Dad hardly ever showed any strong emotion, let alone something as negative as anger.

Another time, after Dad told me that after high school he had hoped to attend college in Bozeman but couldn't afford it, I had a question.

"What about after the war, Dad, couldn't you have gone on the GI bill?"

"I wanted to, but the ranch wasn't making any money and someone had to keep cash coming in. I'd sent them my navy pay, but I think they used that for Byron's tuition at the U. He was always smarter than me; I guess the squeaky wheel got the grease."

As brothers, Walter and Byron were very different. Byron was loud and sure of himself, always ready with an opinion presented as fact. Dad was quiet, almost shy, and thought before he spoke or acted.

"So what did you do?"

"I took a job in 1947, running a crew of painters back in Hawaii. I got hepatitis there and I was sick for over a year. I almost died. It would have been better for everybody if I had."

When Dad talked like that it was a sign he was depressed.

"I sure am lucky you didn't. Being on the ranch with you probably saved my life. You taught me how to work and showed me how to behave. You know I see people at the food pantry, some of them drunks and addicts, who probably aren't ever going to get any better."

"Oh Douglas, I could have done better with you. I made so many mistakes."

It was hard for Dad to accept a compliment, another trait he passed on to me.

We also talked about the war. I already knew some basic details about his time in the navy. I knew he had served as a pharmacist mate first class, assigned to the 4th Marine Division. I knew he made amphibious landings with them on four islands in the Pacific and received Silver and Bronze stars. I also knew that whatever happened on those four islands - Roi-Namor, Saipan, Tinian and Iwo Jima – had nearly destroyed him.

He had a lot of wartime memories, but as he aged, three specific incidents seemed locked in a sort of feedback loop in his mind. On Saipan he was bandaging a wounded marine when an artillery shell exploded close enough to knock him out and he remembers waking up 'Swearing a blue streak.'

On Tinian he was awarded the Silver Star for grabbing a jeep and rescuing a wounded man while under active sniper fire after the jeep driver had refused.

On Iwo Jima he and another man ran with a stretcher while they dodged machine gun fire. A little later, while searching for wounded in a ravine, he came face to face with a Japanese officer. Dad hurled a grenade in lieu of shooting because "I never could hit anything with a pistol."

Other mornings I told him more about some of the clients I saw at the food pantry, their pitiful lives and how little hope many of them had that anything would ever get better.

"I am so lucky, Dad, I should have died a half-dozen times. Thanks for sticking by me."

"I see more and more people like that at the church, a lot of them with drug or mental problems. I can't help them. All I can do is keep giving to the church."

"I can't help them either, Dad, and sometimes I wonder why I try."

"Your remind me of Jerry when you talk like that. You know she was always trying to help people. Do you remember Donny Wilson from the church?"

"A little bit. He was handicapped, right?"

"Mentally, yes, physically he could just about take care of himself. He even had a part time job as a janitor but he could barely read and couldn't pay bills or anything like that. He got a little social security and with the job he could have done okay. But his family was no good. They took all his money and spent it on alcohol. It made your mother so mad. She went before a judge and got declared his guardian. She set up a bank account for him, paid his bills, kept his family from stealing his checks. She found him a place of his own, a little studio apartment downtown so he could walk to work."

"I didn't know about any of that, Dad." Was this the same woman I fought with for years?

"Donnie loved Jerry. I remember him at her funeral, how lost he looked. Then I found out that before she died, she had recruited someone else to take over what she did."

"I had no idea mom ever did anything like that."

"She did other stuff too. Do you remember that busted up cowboy we brought home?"

"I haven't thought of him in forever, Dad, but I do remember. I was nine or ten, and this old guy had showed up at church. Didn't he have dinner with us?" I questioned.

"That's right. Jerry got to talking with him after the service and felt sorry. Later after we ate I gave him a grub-hoe and walked him down to the horse pasture where there was a huge patch of bull thistles. He didn't get much done, too sick I guess. I could smell the whiskey coming off him. A couple hours later I drove him back to town and gave him ten dollars."

"That was good money back then. He probably spent it on a fifth. It must have been hard for the Scot in you." I teased.

"Well, your mother insisted. She had a soft heart for broken people, I guess."

"I didn't see that side of her, not when it came to my mistakes," I said.

"She just expected more from you, Douglas. Anyway, I couldn't talk to people the way she did; still can't. All I can give is money."

"Maybe I'm more like her than I thought. It's hard though, you know, like leading a horse to water and then it tries to bite you."

Dad laughed. "You won't give up, though, will you?"

"No I won't. Guess I'm almost as stubborn as Mom."

"I've wondered about something else for a long time, Douglas." I could hear him take a deep breath and exhale. "Why can some people get sober and others just can't? I served with a corpsman named DeVore. He was real smart, he could talk his way out of anything. But if he took one drink, he couldn't stop. We'd go on liberty together sometimes. If I was with him he didn't drink."

"Maybe he wasn't ready." I didn't have a real answer for him. We'd never had exchanges like this before; about misery, our proper response, and the question of giving up. I could visualize him on the other end of the call, shaking his head in bafflement, and laughing, almost, at our vain attempts to change or even understand the human condition.

Week, by month, by year, I observed his decline. In 2013, he bought his last new car and, though he continued to drive until his ninety-sixth birthday, it became more and more difficult.

Nancy kept me current on his health and the state of his memory, two things he seldom mentioned.

Twice a year Joan and I drove or flew to Missoula. From my youth, I remember him as always standing erect, but now he hunched under the weight of years, and the heavy work that had been his life on the ranch. Even so, his grip was powerful and his arm strength amazing. His mind seemed sharp, his memory as good as mine. He loved company, and would rise to the occasion when anyone came to the door.

In 2014, Dad suffered another loss when Tess, succumbed to cancer. Dad and Lee had both loved birds and waged an unrelenting war on the hordes of squirrels that plundered their bird feeders. For ten years Tess had cleared the yard of squirrels with a bloodthirsty efficiency. A replacement dog proved disinterested in squirrels and so another piece of his happiness vanished.

In the summer of 2016, Dad fell in the backyard and injured his foot. By now our Saturday conversations were harder for us both. Dying is not something most of us like to discuss. We know we have to die, so we prepare for death. Dad decided he would die at home, so he and Nancy prepared. All his affairs were in order. Nancy had power of attorney and Dad had already set up a Revocable Trust Agreement to avoid probate. Dad had selected a coffin, paid for a burial site, and transferred ownership of his house and car to Nancy.

Dad had a DNR order from the same doctor who had approved hospice care. The VA provided four hours of in-home care a week, and the pharmacy delivered Dad's meds to his door. He had been using a walker for some months and with the aid of a lift recliner, he could move from chair, to walker to bathroom by himself.

Life has a way of confounding our best laid plans. Dad's fall in the yard was like that. For several days after he fell, Dad remained in bed without eating. During that time he lost strength, his intestines stopped working and he experienced a lot of pain. Severe constipation required laxatives. Laxatives produced diarrhea. His doctor, together with hospice personnel and my sister pulled him through, but he remained weaker than before.

That was the situation on August 24, 2016, when Joan and I started down the Alcan. By the time we arrived in Missoula he seemed stable, and, although I lobbied for hiring additional caregivers, Dad didn't want to spend the money, so we didn't. Joan and I drove back to Homer before the end of September with the understanding that I would fly down if I was needed.

Within a week, Dad fell several more times trying to make his way to the bathroom. When Nancy couldn't get him off the floor, she called the fire department. The VA agreed, somewhat grudgingly, to pay for twenty-four additional hours of care each week but the home care service they suggested only had staff for four hours and Nancy struggled to care for Dad alone. It wasn't working, so I flew down right away.

At first, I was able to assist him to the toilet and shower, but as he weakened, his one hundred eighty-five pounds became more than I could manage. With Nancy's consent, I fired the care agency the VA had suggested and found another. They had adequate staff but it took us a week to make all the schedule changes and provide Walter with the coverage he needed.

For that week Nancy and I took turns sleeping and did our best. Dad spent much of that time sitting in his recliner since we couldn't move him ourselves. Three mornings a week, a hospice bath aid arrived and the three of us got him cleaned and changed. Weekends we called on friends and family for aid. I felt helpless, angry, and guilty. Helpless, because I couldn't give Dad the care he needed; angry, because his stubborn frugality had put us on the spot; and guilty, because of my anger. Exhausted and helpless, I berated myself: what would people think of a son who allowed his father to suffer like this? Apparently, I truly am my mother's son..

On October 25, 2016, six days after his ninety-eighth birthday, Dad died at home, surrounded by people he loved. The subsequent military service at graveside was limited to close family as he had requested. After taps, and a salute from the VFW, I stood in the chill, spattering, rain and read aloud.

"Throughout his life Walter Dodd put the needs of others above his own desires. Grinding poverty on a hardscrabble ranch during the Great Depression, kept him from college. Instead he went from work to war and back to work – but he never became bitter, and I was blessed when he entered my life in 1951. He was a hard worker who loved to play but seldom had the time; a quiet man of strong opinions and deep faith who chose not to talk about politics, religion or money. He seldom raised his voice and never raised a hand against me, despite my many transgressions. He avoided gossip. He was the living definition of integrity; his verbal promise better than many a man's signed contract.

He had a head full of stories that he loved to share. Here is one about him:

One August afternoon, while putting new shoes on our horse, Jiggs, Dad came in to the house and sat down on the couch. I was astounded because he never, ever came into the house in mid- afternoon. After a few minutes, he went back outside, finished with Jiggs, came in, and addressed my mother:

'Jerry, we need to go to town.'

The two of them got in the Plymouth wagon and, with my mother driving, vanished down the road in a cloud of dust. When they returned hours later Dad was on crutches with a full leg cast. Jiggs had put his foot down suddenly on Dad's leg and snapped the bone.

The broken leg came just after Dad had started laying the walls of a two-story, concrete block house for his parents. A family photo album from that period shows a picture of him crawling on a scaffold, holding a cement block, still wearing the cast. Underneath the picture, written in Dad's steady hand, are these words 'Laying the last block and I'm still in full leg cast October 1st 1957'. Is that look on his face simply satisfaction, or perhaps perverse enjoyment? I asked Dad that question about a month ago and he just laughed."

When I finished reading, the honor guard folded the flag and presented it to me. The wind through the cemetery was cold and held the promise of snow. By now, everyone was chilled but hesitant to be the first to leave. Joan and I walked to our car and drove to the church. The church was warm and the service was well attended. Nancy sang and the minister delivered a eulogy. Then, as Walter would have wished, the crowd gathered in the fellowship hall where we ate and shared stores. Walter was gone, but everyone there remembered him, and we were alive.

Chapter 41

Full Circle

January, 2017 Homer

The gale off the bay blasts sleet against the windows of the Methodist church - typical January weather for Homer - and in the daylight basement, water pools on the floor and clothing steams as people wait for one o'clock. The line runs from the table where Dave and I sit, across the room, out the double doors and into the packed entryway. Friends greet each other; for some these Monday afternoons may be their week's social highlight. There are newcomers, too, like the mother gazing vacantly into space as her three small children jostle a legless old man in a wheelchair. Behind him, a clot of ragged, scruffy-bearded men in their twenties joke with each other as they swirl around an immensely fat woman slumped against her walker. Behind her, a native man of indeterminate age stands silently, head down. Some carry backpacks, cloth shopping bags, or cardboard boxes.

"Lot of customers today, Dave," I offer as he opens his laptop.

"Yeah, but nowhere close to the one-sixty we had on Christmas, probably less than a hundred. We have a lot of food so it shouldn't be a problem."

"Yeah, it was great to get that big Coast Guard donation."

The line moves forward as Dave checks off names in the computer.

"This is my first time here. How does this work?" Dirty-faced with a baby on her hip, the girl peers hesitantly at Dave out of a ragged, oversized hooded Carhartt sweatshirt.

"What's your name and birthday, and how many in your household?" Dave asks.

"Lisa Jones, April twenty-second, 1999, and it's just me and him," she replies, indicating the baby with a nod.

"Okay, Lisa, take this ticket," Dave hands her a small square of cardboard marked with a bold number 2, "and get in line over there. Show that when it's your turn, and they'll explain everything. Oh, ask them to sign you up for a CSFP box too." Seeing her blank look, Dave continues.

"That's the surplus commodity program for seniors and single moms. Also, since it's your first time here you can get some rice, beans and canned goods if you want."

Lisa just stands there. She looks bewildered and about twelve years old. I sigh. Babies having babies. What kind of future will there be for her and her son? I get to my feet and offer what I hope is a reassuring smile.

"Come on, Lisa, I'll walk you over to the food."

Lisa follows me out the door, through the entryway, past the line of waiting clients, and through another door that opens into the atrium that serves as the church's fellowship room. Inside, long folding tables line the walls. The first table holds juice, eggs, dairy items and ready to eat lunches packed in to-go boxes. The next two tables bear vegetables - onions, potatoes, carrots, cabbage, lettuce and more exotic things like jalapeños and artichokes. There is a fruit table, and three more tables piled high with bread, bagels, cookies, pies, and cakes. A final table is labeled 'at risk' and holds a variety of opened packages and other items whose provenance is in question. Two large coolers contain frozen fish and meat.

The scene is one of barely controlled chaos. All food pantry workers are volunteers and trying to force them to operate like a smooth, well-oiled, machine is like trying to persuade a herd of cats to put toothpaste back in a tube. At each section, a volunteer waits, making sure all the clients get their share of the food. To our regulars this bounty is no surprise, but Lisa stops, gaping, rooted in place. I motion her farther into the room and up to the first table.

"Hey, Anita, this is Lisa. She's never been here before. Can you walk her through this?"

"Sure thing, Doug. Come on, honey, let's start right here. Oh my, what a cute baby. What's his name?" With Lisa in good hands, I leave the atrium and head back to my room.

Some people assume that since we're called a food pantry, all we do is hand out food, but the truth is more complicated. At the pantry we see people from all kinds of situations with every imaginable problem. They are of every age, race and gender. We see the working poor, the single parents, the emotionally and psychologically handicapped, and those with huge medical expenses. There is the widow, the orphan and the addict in our midst. Some clients just want to walk in, get a voucher for a shower or gasoline, and walk out. Others arrive with problems that seem totally overwhelming. Some don't know what they need or even want. These people are my clients

On a given Monday afternoon, we may have four or a dozen clients requesting more than food. What with looking up client histories, verifying their documentation, recording new data, problem solving solutions, filling out vouchers and writing checks, there is a lot to do. All these routine tasks are more than I can handle myself. Fortunately Nadya is there to help me.

Together we do a lot of listening. People need to be heard and acknowledged and some of our clients have grown used to being ignored, to becoming invisible. You may have seen them, shabbily dressed men and women sitting in libraries, standing on the streets or sleeping on the grass in parks. In our job listening is a requirement lest we become vending machines with legs.

Nadya and I have done this together for over two years and by now we make a good team. When a client comes in crying and leaves laughing – which happens more often than you might expect – I know we have done well. When everything turns to shit despite our best efforts – which happens less often than I might fear – Nadya and I can debrief the encounter, pick each other up, and move on.

On this particular Monday we have a scheduled client who should be waiting but I've learned that rather than make appointments I might as well put up a sign reading 'Walk-ins Welcome'. Nadya is waiting for me when I return..

"They put some guy in our room," she says, "never seen him before, no idea what he wants."

"Thanks, we'll figure it out," I respond.

Nadya and I enter the small, windowless interview room, and as I close the door, the stink of an unwashed body, mixed with wood smoke and the stale aroma of alcohol, slaps me in the face. My sense of smell has never completely recovered from the radiation treatments I endured in 2008, but sometimes that is a good thing.

At the table I see myself from twenty years ago. He wears a greasy stocking cap and at least four layers of clothing. A ragged, blackened backpack lies behind him on the floor. His dark hair is shaggy and I glimpse raw sores underneath his beard and on the back of his hands. He looks to be about fifty, but is almost certainly younger. Homeless, I guess. Probably couch surfing, or squatting in an abandoned dry cabin, or maybe camping in the brush behind Safeway.

"Hi, I'm Doug and this is Nadya." I put out my hand.

"Uh, Willie," he mutters, studiously avoiding my gaze. I wait, and as he finally takes my hand I can feel a slight tremor.

"Good to meet you, Willie," I smile. "So what's up?"

"I don't have nowhere to stay and they told me you guys give out hotel vouchers." His tone is defensive, almost angry, but I see misery in his face.

"Sometimes. It depends. How come you have no place to stay?"

"I hitchhiked down from Anchorage a couple weeks ago and the guy who gave me a ride let me sleep in one of his sheds. But there's no heat and no insulation. I'm 'bout to freeze to death there." His eyes are dull, his words rote, as though he's repeated them many times.

"Do you have a photo ID?" Nadya asks. Willie digs in a pocket and finally produces a scratched, barely legible Alaska ID card. The picture could be his from a better time.

"So," I calculate, "you'll be 39 in March. That right?"

"Yeah, I guess," he replies.

"Why did you come to Homer, Willie? I ask.

"There's no work in Anchorage and it's not safe. People there will stab you for a pack of smokes."

"Compared to Homer, Anchorage has a lot of jobs, especially in the winter. What are you planning to do here to get squared away? How are you going to live?"

"I'll get a job on a boat or in the cannery."

"You ever worked on a boat?"

"Not exactly."

"Look, most skippers hire somebody they know or at least a guy with experience." Willie starts to interrupt and I hold up a finger. "Also nobody's fishing right now – cod won't start till the end of the month – so there's no processor work either. Where do you plan to stay for the next month?"

"That's why I need the voucher," he whines.

"Here are some facts of life, Willie. Our money comes from private donations and we can only help each person up to $250 a year. The cheapest hotel in Homer right now is $300 for one week, so even if we help you, a week later you'll be right back where you are now. Frankly, that's a waste of our money and it won't solve your problem. How much money do you have?"

"I got nothing."

"What about your PFD? That was over a thousand bucks this year." I let the silence stretch for a bit. It has been three months since most Alaska residents received their annual cash dividend from the state, and I want to hear what Willie has done with his. During this entire conversation Nadya has been silently working at the computer. Willie's name and basic information is now on file along with his request and perhaps her observations. All this will be useful should Willie pay us a return visit.

"The damned state took it. Said I had some fines. Took it all."

"I guess you've got a real problem then. But if you're broke, where did you get the booze I smell?" He slumps with his head down, not answering.

"Look, Willie, problems are like monkeys. You have a monkey and you're looking for somebody to adopt it. We don't want your monkey. Unless you're ready to get honest about this you're just wasting your time and mine." He fidgets in his chair and I let the silence build again.

"People like you, you got no idea what it's like," he bursts out. "You think I like being homeless and living like this? Aren't you supposed help people? Aw screw it, you never been on the street, you wouldn't understand." Willie makes as if to rise.

"I was homeless for over two years, Willie," I say sharply. "I was an addict too, so you can save the 'poor me' and your BS excuses. What's your real story?"

"All right, damn it! Don't you think I know I'm a fuck-up?" He looks at Nadya, and perhaps realizing that he is in a church basement in the presence of a woman, reddens and manages a muted "I'm Sorry." before continuing: "Look, I got nothin' 'cause I am nothin' – 'cept a junkie and a drunk. I left Anchorage after I stole some meth from a guy and I knew he'd kill me if he caught me." His voice cracks and I see the beginning of real desperation in his moist eyes.

"Any legal problems, Willie?" Nadya asks, her tone soft, "Are there any wants out on you?"

"I don't think so. Like I said, I owe child support but that's it."

"We can't afford to put you in a hotel," I resume, "but there is a possibility. A church here runs a small bunkhouse for men. They have a zero tolerance policy for drugs and alcohol. Do you think you could stay sober there?"

"I don't much like churches. Damn preachers just want your money."

"You're sitting in a church basement right now, out of the snow and wind, and you're the one asking for money. Can you stay sober; at least for a little while?"

"Sorry, man, I'm just stressed. I don't mean no disrespect. I can stay sober for a while, I done it before. I really need to get cleaned up, but no church is gonna want anything to do with me."

"You'll be surprised. This church is different. Everyone is welcome. Pastor Darren has ink, lifts weights and rides a Harley. They have a bunkhouse right on the church property with a shower, washer and dryer. Got a kitchen all the men share. Only thing is, if you do get drunk they *will* ask you to leave, so you better have a plan. There are two or three AA meetings every day a few blocks from the church. You ever go to AA?"

"I tried the AA stuff once, stayed clean for a month. It sucks but I can do it. What does this bunkhouse cost?"

"The bunkhouse is $300 a month. You can pay $150 and work off the rest by doing jobs around the church. We can pay for the first month; after that it'll be up to you, so you'll need to get a job. If you find one on a boat, great; but in case you can't, you should try other places. My brother has a restaurant and he may need a dishwasher. You can get a clothing voucher at the Salvation Army and get cleaned up. Are you willing to give it a try?"

"Yeah, okay. I'm sick and tired of living like this." Willie meets my gaze. "Thanks."

"No problem, let me call Pastor Darren, make sure they have a bed." I pick up my phone and press one key. As I wait, I look at Willie and wonder at his chances.

"Hey Darren, you still got that bed open? Good. Listen, I got a guy here I want to send you, goes by Willie. Thanks, I'll get a check up to you later. Bless you too."

"Okay Willie, you got a chance. Try not to blow it, okay?"

"Thanks, you guys, I appreciate it."

"You're welcome. One thing: before you go, I need to tell you a story about a ram and a porcupine."

AFTERWARD

So, now we have a happy ending, right? Willie or Bob or the latest bum-of-the-week, goes to meetings, stops drinking and drugging, and his life changes. It would be pretty to think so – and it's not impossible. People get sober every day. Somebody wins the lottery. However, I'm not waiting for that day or searching for that somebody. My story is not typical, and most fifty-five year old junkies never recover.

Too many shelters close down or don't have beds and the cops find too many addicts dead, their rigs still in their arms. Oh, I'll probably keep telling stories about porcupines and slapping Band-Aids on sucking chest wounds. Maybe I'll even get better at it. I'm not doing it because I expect it to work. I'm doing it because it needs to be done and people did it for me; and besides Band-Aids and porcupines are what I have.